Volume One

BRITISH RAILWAYS
ROAD VEHICLES
1948-1968

Alan Earnshaw

&

Bill Aldridge

Trans-Pennine Publishing

CONTENTS

The **Nostalgia Road** Series ™
is conceived, designed and published
by
Trans-Pennine Publishing Ltd.
PO Box 10
Appleby-in-Westmorland
Cumbria, CA16 6FA
Tel. 017683 51053
Fax. 017683 53558
ISDN. 017683 53684
e-mail trans.pennine@virgin.net
(A Quality Guild registered company)

Reprographics
Barnabus Design & Repro
Threemilestone, Truro
Cornwall, TR4 9AN
01872 241185

And Printed in Cumbria by
Kent Valley Colour Printers Ltd.
Shap Road Industrial Estate
Kendal, Cumbria LA9 6NZ
01539 741344

Front Cover: *Seen at the National Railway Museum's Railways & Roads Event in August 1998, this Thornycroft Nippy tractor unit and trailer has the honour to be one of the first vehicles to use the (then) recently restored weighbridge. Registered JXA 392, the Thornycroft is painted in the carmine and cream livery with Eastern Region markings.* **Alan Earnshaw**

Rear Cover Top: *Taken in the mid-1950s, this picture shows a Fordson D series lorry at Clayton West Station (in the West Riding of Yorkshire). Working on the country lorry delivery service from the branch terminus, driver Basil Clegg is pictured with his faithful sheepdog that accompanied him on his rounds.* **Phil Roberts.**

Rear Cover Bottom: *The final fling of the railway-owned road delivery fleet is captured in the late-1960s, as a former BR Scammell Townsman is seen at Wembley in National Carriers livery.* **Bill Aldridge**

Title Page: *Yet another Thornycroft Nippy from the same batch of vehicles as that pictured on the cover, this time JXA 400 which was D8578 in the Western Region fleet.*

This Page: *A relatively rare make in the BR road vehicle fleet was the Sentinel marque, as this is a firm more commonly associated with steam lorries. However they did build internal combustion engined commercials, and here we have OYL 466, which is engaged on insulated container duties with the Southern Region.*

© Trans-Pennine Publishing & Alan Earnshaw/Bill Aldridge 1996, 2001
Photographs: As credited

INTRODUCTION

This is the first volume of the **Famous Fleets** series, and thus an important part of the Nostalgia Road story. In the volumes that follow we intend to tell the story of how some of Britain's best-known fleets developed their businesses. Yet not only will we tell the story of large private operators, but we will also recall the history of nationally operated fleets, as for example the NHS Ambulance Service.

Many of the fleets we will consider in the series are still with us today (or at least their names are), even though the types of vehicles, services and liveries have changed dramatically during the past half-century. When it comes to manufacturing company fleets, we have the added complication that the actual vehicles might have been owned by a sub-contractor and only painted in the livery of the manufacturers. Nevertheless, some of the names on the sides of today's lorries, buses and vans are those which we can associate with the highway scene back in the 1950s and '60s, and yet they have endured to remain with us into the 21st Century. Some are but distant memories, and included in this category is one of the largest road vehicle fleets ever operated in Great Britain. It is this fleet, the one operated by British Railways, with which we start our series.

Arguably the most important road delivery fleets at the end of World War II were those that belonged to the four main-line railway operators, which (at the time) were amongst the biggest joint-stock companies in the world. The Great Western (GWR), London Midland & Scottish (LMS), London & North Eastern (LNER) and Southern (SR) railways were, however, merged into British Railways through the Transport Act 1947 when it came into effect on 1st January 1948.

Above: *In the mid-1940s, the LMS bought a fleet of Bedford OSS tractor units as part of its plan to update the road service, one of these (GRO 684) is seen here. Bearing fleet number 3695BG-M, the tractor unit looks splendid in its British Railways livery, as it carries a replica of Stephenson's* Rocket *on a step frame trailer to an exhibition in Derby.* BR LMR

At the time of its conception, British Railways had the largest general delivery vehicle fleet in Europe, possibly the world. It was a massive operation, and one which should have been with us down to today as part of an integrated road-rail freight operation. Sadly, it lasted just 20 years as a whole. Thereafter it was hived off to other operators, many of which eventually became private sector firms.

This book sets out to tell the story of the rise and fall of the state-owned railway road vehicle operation in Britain during that 20 year period, and it is intended to be the first of five books discussing the whole railway-road transport scene between 1923 and 1968.

In looking at its constituent parts we have not aimed to give a vehicle by vehicle description, for the primary reason that far too many types of lorry and van were employed during the period concerned. Rather we have endeavoured to categorise the types of road vehicle operations undertaken by BR, with the exception of civil engineering vehicles, which is another story altogether - although we do present some views of railway service vehicles in this book.

As its title implies, this book deals with the 'road delivery vehicles' used by British Railways and our objective in this instance is to look specifically at those that can be loosely termed 'revenue earning'.

However, we have to use the term 'revenue-earning' very advisedly because, as we will show, BR's road delivery fleet lost substantial sums of money during its 20 years of operation. We must also look closely at what was happening on the railways over the years, particularly 1955-6, as this can be said to be the turning point in the entire story. How the Suez Crisis (and its subsequent petrol rationing) should have been the turning point in the failing fortunes of the road delivery fleet is discussed in a chapter on its own, and like many facts in this book it does not make happy reading.

Despite the sad story that underlines the demise of this once great fleet, our book will present a powerful picture of the diversity of the BR road fleet. Since it was first published in 1997 it has become a minor work of reference, and has been invaluable to both road vehicle and railway modellers. Yet it has also had a much wider appeal, in that it told the fascinating story of a little-discussed, yet massive road vehicle fleet. As this book now goes to a revision and re-print, we are completing the manuscript for the book *LMS Railway Road Vehicles 1923-1947*.

This is the second of our 'Big Four' road vehicles books, following the release of *GWR Road Vehicles* last year. In the not too distant future, books on the LNER and the Southern Railway road vehicle fleets will also have been produced in order to complete the set. It is then hoped that we can turn our attention to British Railway Buses & Personnel Carriers, and also those vehicles used by the Civil Engineering and Permanent Way departments.

Along with the rest of our Famous Fleet books, we have designed these railway-road vehicle titles to be of interest to a broad-band audience, but despite their small size, they should not be dismissed as light-weight paperbacks, for they are intended to be moderately priced informative works of reference.

Like the rest of the Nostalgia Road series, these books are designed to play an important role in recording the great days of British motoring. This book has already sold right around the world, so Bill and I hope you will enjoy this expanded volume.

Alan Earnshaw   Appleby, February 2001

The Great Bridge Street depot in Birmingham, with a LAD-cabbed Dodge being loaded with an open steel coil container. Note the BRS Atkinson behind the crane, as it awaits the next load. This picture is an example of what could be achieved by an integrated national transport system. BR-LMR

RAILWAY OWNED ROAD VEHICLES

Above: *At the end of World War I, the railways found it worthwhile to purchase war surplus petrol-engined lorries. Pictured in Holmfirth c.1920 a Lancashire & Yorkshire Railway Peerless (ex-American Army) lorry carries bales of wool to the town's station.*

As 1st January 1948 dawned, Britain awoke expecting a new era from the public ownership of the nation's transport system. Yet, despite the amount of planning that the Labour government had put into the nationalisation of the railways, the only outward sign of change was the alteration of some logos on a few of the locomotives or the nameplates at headquarters. As far as the goods operation was concerned, the New Year of 1948 faced just the same problems that the railways had suffered since the war ended in the summer of 1945.

The main problems were lack of investment, lack of maintenance and lack of new equipment. All of which was coupled with a surfeit of competition from the road hauliers who could often run rings around the desperately important yet somewhat moribund railway goods operation. Nationalisation brought little to write home about, except a rigid approach by both management and staff. Furthermore, the bureaucratic attitude of a Government-controlled body, coupled with the growing militantism of the railway unions, gave very little consideration for what the customer needed. But who were the railway's freight customers, and what did they need?

The answer to this question is both long and complex, but basically we can show that movement of goods by the railways could be broken down into four separate parts, with very little overlap. Firstly, we had the movement of bulk freight. This was normally sent in full train-loads, from producer to consumer and rarely needed transhipment from the rail vehicles into which the consignments were first loaded; for example, bulk movements of coal from mines to power stations or gas works. Secondly, in terms of revenue at least, came the freight moved in full wagon loads, such as steel or timber. This type of traffic, although originating from a single despatch point, was often bound for different destinations. As a result it would have to be handled at a variety of places along the rail network. The journey from the originating station, might see the goods pass through several marshalling/goods yards before delivery, and would often involve a final movement by road vehicle.

Top Left: *Outside Meltham station is one of the delivery lorries of Earnshaw & Sons, who were cartage agents for the Lancashire & Yorkshire Rly between 1868 and 1924. Pictured sitting on the flat-bed lorry (around the year 1892) is my grandfather Ai Earnshaw.*

Bottom Left: *By the 1920s many of the agencies had been taken over by the railways themselves, and this horse-drawn wagon in Bristol is fairly typical of the period. However, the position of car-man was traditionally a male-only job. But this picture was taken in October 1940 when labour was at a premium. Even so, Miss Vera Proctor is thought to be the only woman (in the entire West Country) who was occupied in this type of work at the time.* LMS Official

The third category of goods was known as sundries or 'smalls' traffic, and generally consisted of consignments varying between 2lbs and 1-ton. This traffic was directed through depots where the individual consignments would be grouped together in rail vans for the trunk portion of the journey, it would then be re-sorted at the destination depot for delivery to the consignee. Fourth, and finally, came the express parcels traffic. This was generally moved on passenger trains and enjoyed its own dedicated collection and delivery network.

However, by the end of World War II the railway freight operation was suffering from the serious effects of under-funding and over-work, so there was a ready and willing market place for firms who could offer alternate services. Rapid, more effective shipment of goods was especially important as the country benefited from full employment.

One of the remarkable facts concerning the scope of the railway operation at the time of nationalisation, was the fact that 85% of coal supplies were moved by rail as was up to 55% of consumer goods. Accordingly, a huge infrastructure existed to support this operation. This included almost 12,000 road vehicles and 7,404 horses, which were inherited by BR on 1st January 1948. This combined road fleet carried about 28 million tons of traffic which was roughly 10% of the total railway goods tonnage, but a further 4 million tons was still carried by BR agents and contractors.

The 1947 Transport Act, which set up the nationalisation process required BR to reduce the cartage facilities (presumably meaning vehicle numbers), and thereafter rely on British Road Services to supply any additional requirements such as seasonal work. It is doubtful that this part of the Act was ever really implemented, since the cartage facilities remained much the same as in the past, when the railways had simply hired outside vehicles to cover traffic peaks.

For the full train load traffic, which was generally bulk goods, there were established facilities and little effective competition. Wagon load traffic was still high, but it was vulnerable to the road hauliers. The sundries/cartage and smalls traffic was comprehensively handled through a nation-wide network of over 4,700 depots. It offered a delivery and collection service for goods in this less than wagon load category at competitive transit rates. However, it was not at all profitable, for (in 1948) the working expenses amounted to £12 million, but the receipts only reached £8 million.

An integrated transport system, such as had been legally imposed in Britain during the war was seen as being the only answer to the nation's post-war troubles. Consequently, the first post-war Labour government set about the creation of such a system, with all the railways, docks, airports, road haulage and canals coming under State-control. To oversee this integrated system, the Government appointed a controlling and regulatory body, the British Transport Commission (BTC).

Nationalisation seemed a good idea, but it soon emerged that there were far too many problems concerning the internal structure of the BTC. These problems had a cumulative effect on this transport policy in general, with a 'knock-on result' for the constituent parts of the BTC operation in particular! Within its short life the BTC failed miserably in its attempts to bring about major improvements, and it blamed price restraints on its rapidly increasing deficits! Yet its failure had more to do with blinkered vision than past problems. No senior executive was willing to face the obvious and note that the gradual disappearance of freight was a reflection on the validity of pre-war practices on the post-war transport market. Even so, the next incoming government (Conservative) had no solutions either, and they simply abolished the nationalised road industry, replacing it with a free market operation.

Whilst de-nationalisation in 1953 left the parcels division of BRS relatively intact, it was free of the restraints of overall control in an integrated transport system. It therefore became a serious competitor to BR's road vehicle operations. Yet, with the demise of the BTC, there were some advantages for the railways, as it enabled the decision-making process to be handled further down the BR management structure. It even took tentative steps towards abolishing the railway's common carrier obligation which had been requested before the war.

The Tories later introduced the BR Modernisation Plan, but it is generally accepted that it had glaring faults. These included a total lack of foresight and a general assumption that, by sorting out problems that had been annoying rail managers since before the war, they could bring the standards of operating up to meet the needs of modern businesses.

Top Right: *During World War I, several railway workshops gained experience in manufacturing motor lorries for the army - for example the L&YR's Newton Heath Works near Manchester, produced no less than 11 lorries a day for Leyland Motors.* National Railway Museum

Centre Right: *In the 1930s the railways regularised their bus services, merging or absorbing bus firms that had previously been competitors. In some areas they also entered 'joint' agreements with municipal undertakings like Huddersfield Corporation (the first council in the world to operate a public bus service). This view shows Joint Omnibus Committee No. 2, a 20 seat Leyland Cub with Roe body-work before entering regular service.* Charles H. Roe Ltd.

Bottom Right: *Some 50 years on from the previous picture at Meltham, progress has been made with the railway's delivery fleet, as a Scammell 6-ton Mechanical Horse collects a David Brown VAK1 tractor from the factory at Meltham Mills.* David Brown Tractors

Above: *Although still bearing its LMS livery this Karrier Bantam GRO185 (Fleet No. 1223-D) was actually photographed in Cheshire some five and a half years after nationalisation had taken place. Seen at Congleton station on 20th June 1953, along with a horse-drawn dray M24244 (Wolverton 1936), this picture is not an isolated view of an antiquated service at rural stations, but is quite representative of what was being used in the late 1940s and early 1950s.* F.W. Shuttleworth

Below: *Another inherited vehicle, is this Bedford K type, OAR 288, which was turned out from Vauxhall's factory in Luton in October 1947. Purchased by the LMS as a chassis-cowl (that is to say without cab or body), delivery was made to Derby works, where one presumes the railway company built and fitted the body. With the fleet number M1676D M, denoting its pre-BR ownership, the van is seen on collection work in the East Midlands when it was around eight years old.* F. Cassell

Under normal circumstances no commercially-driven business could have ever sustained the high losses that BR endured, but it is important to remember that the railways had always treated the road operation purely as a means to an end. To them this was an ancillary service, which allowed the real profit to be made on the rail portion of the journey, therefore they could overlook this particular recurring loss. In their favour was the fact that there were few road hauliers who could then offer the type of a country-wide delivery and collection coverage for small loads that was given by the railway lorry operation.

Actually, in 1950 BR stated, somewhat over-confidently (and certainly prematurely), that 'competition from the independent hauliers is substantially under control!' How they came to this rash conclusion is open to speculation, but we must assume it was due partly to the proposed co-ordination between BR and BRS, and partly from the 1933 Road Transport Act that required road hauliers to provide 'proof of need' at the Traffic Courts before they could obtain a licence to operate. In addition, any suppliers of transport services had available to them the 'right of objection' to the grant of a licence to a competitor, and the railways made full use of these powers to keep the hauliers at bay.

There was of course a fly in the ointment in that the 1933 Act had allowed businesses to carry their own goods on their own vehicles. It was not possible for the railways to object to these services, and the growth of these 'own account' fleets remained a thorn in BR's flesh. These own account vehicles running on 'C' licences increased from 304,000 in 1935 to 675,000 in 1949, and to well in excess of one million by the end of 1958. Significantly, by 1960 there were more 'C' and 'C' Contract licensed road vehicles on Britain's road than there were freight vehicles on our railways. By 1950 BR were operating just 6,000 motor vehicles and 18,000 trailers, along with 7,000 horses and 21,500 horse-drawn vehicles. In comparison the Road Haulage Executive ran about 40,000 vehicles including 3,500 former railway vehicles.

The 1962 Transport Act was the last ditch attempt by the Conservative government to improve the railway's desperate financial state. Its given aim was to make management more commercially-minded, and allow the British Railways Board to pick and choose traffic and fix its own charges. Using these new powers, the BRB took steps to stop certain types of established traffic from transferring from rail to road. To do this they introduced several express freight train services between main commercial centres and also routed other freight trains more logically to allow faster transit times. But it was to no avail!

Yet to tell the story of decline, we need to go back in time to first explain the growth of the railway road vehicle fleet. We must return to the 1840s when the individual railways began to offer a door to door collection and delivery service, rather than giving just a simple station to station service. In many cases the road portion of a journey was undertaken by a local cartage agent who was contracted to provide a local collection and delivery service. As early as 1868 my family began providing such a service for the Lancashire & Yorkshire Railway, and they eventually expanded from just one horse-drawn lorry to a fleet of 18 carts and 30 horses within a few years. It was, quite obviously, a highly profitable business if you did it right.

Indeed, there were hundreds of these agents in the early days. While the majority had been taken over by 1948, a few remained in business until the mid-1950s thanks to their having secured 10-year contracts. Many agents lingered on because the railway did not consider it worthwhile to provide their own service, but in most major towns and cities, the railways began operating their own fleets of horses, wagons, drays and vans at an early stage. This fleet was adequate for parcels, luggage, sacks and even sizeable packing cases, but when the railways began offering facilities for the transit of very large or heavy items by rail (such as machinery), a number of traction engines and steam waggons had to be acquired to facilitate the road portion of a journey.

As the wealth of the country grew, more goods came to be moved by rail and the fleets expanded to include members of that newfangled device, the petrol engined goods vehicle. This set the scene for the great changes in railway-owned road transport that would come about with the Grouping in 1923, but the companies were not slow at recognising the challenges that might come from private road hauliers.

Under the 1921 Railway Act, 119 railway companies were amalgamated into just four large joint-stock companies. The newly formed Great Western, London, Midland & Scottish, London & North Eastern, and Southern railways thus became the largest owners of railways, docks and road vehicles in the world. Yet, under the terms of their formation, the railways were obligated to collect and deliver *any* traffic offered to them. Whilst this Act did give the railways permission to refuse to carry a customer's traffic if they did not place all their work with the railways, the 'Big Four' companies never seemed to make full use of this clause.

During the 1920s and 1930s many startling innovations were made to improve services, both on the railways and in areas ancillary to them. For example, considerable expenditure was put into upgrading steamer and ferry services, expanding bus fleets and even developing air transport services - all with the expressed intention of creating an inter-linked and integrated transport service. As a consequence of these prevailing conditions, the railway road-vehicle fleets grew noticeably with a constant move towards both replacing the horse with mechanised transport and offering new services beyond the capabilities of the horse.

When horse-power was the only form of road transport, only those points within a three to five mile radius of a station would be offered a delivery service. However, as the rural roads improved, petrol-engined commercial vehicles were used to open up new services.

One new development was the 'Country Lorry Service', which had a radius of between 7 and 10 miles from a station. It was a major step in extending the railways' sphere of influence, and covered a very large part of the country. Its immediate benefit was to farmers who now had the ability to sell their produce further afield. But the same service was also used for incoming goods, and this led to the setting up of warehousing systems for various manufacturers at rail depots. As a, consequence break-bulk schemes were set up on behalf of numerous retail and wholesale suppliers. These firms were duly encouraged to concentrate traffic for specified areas on a selected centre, with distinct commercial advantages being enjoyed by all concerned.

Above: *The growth of the vehicle fleet was substantial during the early 1950s with over 15,400 motor vehicles and 26,000 trailers in use by 1954. The growth in goods handled also continued with the amount of parcels entering the system increasing to an amazing 147 million, with a further 7 million parcels going through the operations of the cartage agents and BRS as successors to Hays Wharf and Carter Paterson. Of all these figures only a paltry 1% of the traffic was handled throughout by road, with the other 99% being transhipped on and off rail vehicles during the journey. Yet this picture shows the reality of final delivery, and displays a service fraught with hazards that would be tolerated by few firms today. BR-LMR.*

Below: *Even in modern depots, such as the Rail Express Parcels shed seen here at Liverpool, parcels being shipped for the Littlewoods mail order company faced numerous problems due to the volume of traffic being handled. BR-LMR*

Above: *By the time of nationalisation, the poor old horse was completely outmoded, and despite the fact that so many horses were inherited by BR in 1948 they were replaced from most duties as quickly as the delivery of new commercial vehicles would allow. Returning back to Huddersfield once again, we see here the sale of railway horses by auction in June 1948. In 1943 the LMS had been operating 41 horses in the town, by 1947 it was down to 21, and after this sale of eight horses, just six would be left.* Huddersfield Examiner

Below: *The horse drivers always had a great degree of pride in their charges, and annual competitions were held for the best kept horse. Even after the demise of the horse on railway road haulage duties, best kept vehicle competitions were regular highlights in the road operations in the 1950s. Here driver Chadburn of Burton-on-Trent receives an award for his 3-ton Scammell MH.* Bill Aldridge Collection

Under the break bulk schemes, full wagon loads were sent to those centres where the client could use either his own staff or railwaymen to sort the goods. Final delivery was handled on railway lorries, which in certain cases might even be painted in the customer's own livery.

Yet despite all the progress made with railway road services, the early Acts of Parliament authorising railways had not envisaged the movement of goods by road, and it was not until 1928 that they were legally allowed to do so. From this point on the road fleets expanded further by means of either the purchase of new vehicles, or the take-over of both large haulage firms and the small operators who had been cartage agents or sub-contractors. The main intention of these take-overs was to utilise the 'throughout by road' powers granted in the 1928 Act rather than the use of these fleets for collection and delivery work.

Following nationalisation of the road and rail operations in 1948, the fleets of the larger 'acquired' companies (like Pickfords) were passed to BRS, but BR retained all of the cartage agent fleets that the 'Big Four' had taken over. The improvements during the 1920s and 1930s in the ability (and reliability) of both commercial vehicles and the rural road network to handle heavier loads gave the railways many opportunities to obtain new business. A good example is found in the movement of milk to the dairies, either in churns or bulk tanks. As time progressed, dairies were built alongside railway lines and dedicated services sped supplies to the big towns and cities on a daily basis. A similar fast traffic also developed in fruit, vegetables and flowers; for example, flowers gathered in the Channel Isles or the Scillies would be collected from the fields around noon, and arrive at London's Covent Garden Market early enough for wholesaling the following morning.

Despite these obviously advantageous types of business, the biggest problem experienced by the railway companies was the fact that they were classed as 'common carriers'. This meant that they had to accept any type of traffic that was offered to them, and this could include literally anything from diamonds to dinosaur bones. As a result a lot of capital would be tied up in specialist handling and delivery equipment, despite the fact that it may only have been needed just once or twice a year. There was also a serious problem with regard to competition, in that the railway had to publish all its tarrifs. This enabled the road hauliers to undercut the railway's charges by reducing the transport prices on just the types of traffic that suited them, leaving the railways to carry the less profitable items. However, due to their size, the railways were able to combat this to some extent by offering special or preferential rates for certain traffics.

One simple way to match the road hauliers, was for the railways to offer a door to door service without the goods being transhipped in any way. This had been possible since the joint introduction of road/rail compatible containers by the major railway companies in 1928. These containers, built in a bewildering variety of capacities and shapes, had common base sizes and could be easily transhipped between road vehicles and railway wagons. There were other examples too, and all the 'Big Four' companies had established a variety of schemes to further improve levels of service in all sectors of their operations in the years between the two wars, despite the difficult times.

THE EXPRESS PARCELS SERVICE

Perhaps we might accurately call this chapter **HOW TO LOSE MILLIONS**, since this service was one of the biggest examples of transport mismanagement ever experienced in Britain. This was a problem that stemmed from the complexity and size of a potentially lucrative operation that seemed both devoid of central planning and control, coupled to a lack of co-ordination at the sharp end. Despite the endeavours of the dedicated people who were trying to manage or work in the system, there were just too many obstacles set in the way. These issues were further compounded by the greatest difficulty of all - getting someone in authority to make a decision!

It is also strange when you consider that the original road delivery service offered by the railway companies turned out to be the final fling of railway-owned road delivery vehicle operations, so it is perhaps fitting to commence this chapter with a description of the Express Parcels Service. This service comprised the collection and delivery of small parcels from door to door, and was the first work that was won from the horse-drawn stage coaches in the middle of the 19th-century.

Above: *Among the parcel vans operating in Leicester in the 1950s was OAR 786, a Morris Commercial NV series van of 1953 vintage. The Morris is seen here in the company of a Scammell Scarab mechanical horse coupled to a van trailer, both are collecting traffic from Dryads in Leicester, the Morris for the express parcels service and the Scammell for the slower sundries service. Highly efficient perhaps, but two lorries for one parcel?* F. Cassell.

From an early stage the railways found good business in sending parcels by passenger train. Soon they offered dedicated parcels trains, which would carry anything from boxes of flowers to hampers containing the costumes of a theatrical touring company; the railways would also forward it free of charge inside a $1/2$-mile radius of the station (usually by hand-cart)! The express parcels traffic was both wide and varied, but it will probably be best remembered for the Post Office traffic (mail), or the daily newspapers that were sent direct from London to every part of the country. Another important traffic was the delivery of mail-order parcels to private households, with the senders usually requiring next day or second day delivery. All of this combined to help build up a very large operation.

Top Left: *A view of the loading bay at Luton Station in 1962, showing a BR parcel van (fleet No. 1404-DM). This Dennis model was known by the name Triton on the railways, but it looks more like a lightweight Pax IId. Another van working from the station at the same time was a 1954 Karrier Bantam. Interestingly, at the time this picture was taken, both vans carried advertising posters for* Sean Connery in Dr No, *all good clean nostalgic fodder.* P.G. Gomm

Centre Left: *A Fordson Thames integral van, with a radiator grill badge proclaiming 4D. This indicates that the van was one of many BR vehicles powered by the Ford 4-cylinder diesel engine of 3611cc. The Fordson Thames 566E model had been introduced in 1953 and continued in production until 1958, being a normal control model built for a carrying capacity of 3-tons. This van boasted rubber front wings designed to reduce accident damage.*

Bottom Left: *A typical urban environment in Leicester forms the background view for another of the Morris Commercial parcel vans (OAR 817) seen here passing the Corts store in 1963.* F. Cassell

Sadly the Express Parcels Service was an operation which was prone to many failures, and usually did so on traffic that was the most urgent in its nature. Goods sent by passenger train relied on the efficiency of guards to get the consignments off the train at their intended destination, and porters to get it to the collection office. Quite often parcels would over-shoot their station, and at other times they would be off-loaded correctly but lost within the station, or even put on an outgoing train by mistake. A good example of this might be found in 1957, when parts for a 'prototype aero-engine' being sent to RAF Kinross by Ruston Hornsby, 'vanished' after being loaded on to an express at Grantham station. Despite an extensive search by Railway Police and Ministry of Defence personnel, it was ten whole days before the 'secret' parts turned up in the lost property office of Birmingham's New Street Station.

Express Parcels were often of a higher intrinsic value than those carried on the sundries network, and the carriage rates charged on this service generated a higher revenue per parcel. In turn this allowed a dedicated fleet of vehicles and a separate delivery network to operate in the towns and cities; with the vehicles so employed usually having a separate lettering/livery. However, in rural parts of the country, parcels traffic would often be logically delivered by the sundries/cartage fleet.

Latterly, the mainstay of the parcels operation was mail order traffic, and this originated mainly from centres like Bradford, Liverpool, Manchester, Oldham, Sunderland and Worcester. To give an idea of the size of operation, the depot at Oldham alone was despatching around 20,000 parcels a day in the early 1960s. At this time around 88 million express parcels were moving annually by rail. Nearly every one was collected and delivered by road, but the majority of deliveries were just one parcel. Oddly enough, one of the major problems of this time was not the deficiencies in the road delivery fleet, but in the modernisation of the locomotive fleet.

The advent of new forms of traction, whilst improving passenger journeys, actually gave less time for parcels-handling at the stations en-route and as a result more dedicated parcels trains had to be operated. In fact, a parcels concentration depot had been set up at Birmingham Central in 1946 and found to be an ideal resource. Therefore, under BR various schemes to relieve congestion at major stations resulted in plans to build further concentration depots. Amongst these was one at Marylebone, which was designed to reduce the pressure on the existing depots at Euston, St. Pancras and King's Cross. Another example was to be built at Wavertree in Liverpool and when opened, this new centre forwarded 15,000 and received 8,000 daily parcels. Mechanisation was embraced wherever possible, with the use of conveyors and electric trucks to transfer stillages of parcels to the waiting road vans.

Many of the busy delivery drivers had traditionally been given a van boy to assist them, and it was this boy's job to organise the parcels whilst the driver was travelling between calls. For this reason the vans often had direct access into the body from the cab. The van boy was also very useful for preventing thefts from the vans, but the number of van boys diminished as the traffic began to decline.

The express fleet inherited by British Railways included a large number of 1-ton and 30-cwt vans generally of pre-war build. All of the pre-war Dennis and Thornycroft vans were quickly replaced, sometimes with more modern versions of the same manufacturers' offerings. However as cost became more crucial, purchase orders were more often for the cheaper mass-produced chassis. For example, models from the Rootes Group had always proved popular with the railway companies and British Railways continued the tradition by purchasing Commer Q Series vans from 1948 right through all the model changes into the 1970s. The other offering from the Rootes Group stable, the economical Karrier Bantam, also remained very popular in van form.

As late as 1948 some horse-drawn vans were still in use at some locations, as were a number of pre-war electric vans used in the stop-start work in cities. The electric vehicle had featured in the railway fleets from the earliest days of this form of traction despite its drawbacks, and BR continued this tradition by regularly purchasing new models hoping all the time that the latest technology would at last make these silent vans real rivals to the all conquering internal combustion vehicles.

Top Right: *One of a number of experimental battery-electric tractor units being evaluated against the Scarabs; 3031 ME is a 1951 Crompton Parkinson 2.5-ton battery-electric mechanical horse. F. Cassell*

Bottom Right: *At Merthyr Tydfil the BTC decided to implement a new system of self-propulsion, using geared winches and hawsers. The system, engineered by Cowans Sheldon of Carlisle, was devised to replace the old capstan method of the horse era as part of the modernisation programme. As the picture shows, a controlled 'Mane & Tail' type of device was employed to draw rail vans through the depot in an attempt to reduce the amount of shunting by locomotives.*

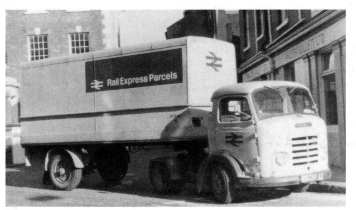

Above: *A replacement for the three-wheel Mechanical Horse was the Karrier Bantam tractor unit, an example of which is seen here in yellow livery on the Sussex coast in 1963. Note the blue and white name panel and the red speed arrows on 863 FJJ (Fleet No. 37218 S).* Peter Love

Below: *The final model of van purchased for the parcel fleet was the famous Commer 'Walk-Thru', a factory built van that had been designed on the American transit-van style. It was able to give a standard of build that was suitable for the multi-stop parcels operation and it was with these vans that the operation finally closed in 1981. The Commer Walk-Thru, was introduced in 1961 but some models were also badged as Karrier, whilst later models were sold with the Dodge name across the short bonnet. Produced by the Rootes Group, by then part of Chrysler, this photograph clearly shows its design had distinct American origins.* British Railways Board.

As an alternative to these vans a number of Austin LD 30-cwt (1.5tonnes) were purchased and these were supplemented by a large fleet of Ford Thames bonneted models, which came in two basic sizes; 2-ton and 3-ton. The only obvious difference between the two was an extended rear overhang on the larger model. The requirements set by BR for these vehicles stated that they should have a good payload space in relation to overall length, yet retain a small turning circle and also have good stability. The cab needed good access from both sides, whilst good ground clearance was a necessity. Additionally due to the restricted nature of some of the collection and delivery points, sliding doors and rubber wings were found to be useful. More often than not the bodies were built in BR's own workshops because the quality and standard of the workmanship could be maintained.

The reasoning behind this was that the railway works were well used to producing high quality, heavy duty, long lasting bodies that would stand up to the vagaries of multi-drop work. Up to the mid-1950s the chassis orders specified, where possible, magneto ignition on petrol engines to reduce the drain on the battery caused by the power consumption of the coil. The average daily distance covered by each van was less than 25 miles and, with the numerous stops and starts, the dynamo had a difficult job keeping the battery fully charged.

Diesel engines were not considered cost-effective at this time, although things were soon to change. One BR executive made a very interesting comment on the quality of engines available at the time by saying 'the high rate of cylinder wear with engines constantly stopping and starting is often underestimated and cylinder liners are regarded by some manufacturers as a refinement rather than something of importance', a rather telling comment on the 'take it or leave it' attitude of vehicle builders at that time. Despite the low mileage and the hesitation of the engineers to get involved with noisy, smelly diesels, the Fordson Thames were thus powered and the fuel savings were so great, that this vehicle alone did enough to make the diesel more popular and they soon became an accepted BR standard.

With its varied fleet, the service shambled through the 1950s and continued in its own inimitable way into the 1960s. That is not to say that the efforts of those involved were in any way open to criticism, it was just that the size of the operation was so vast as to defy good operating procedures. The duplication of effort between the various arms of the road delivery fleet was another problem, and it was not uncommon for an express vehicle to arrive at a customer at exactly the same time as a sundries division lorry. It was often a case of the left hand etc..., but we have to remember that this was in the days before computer generated collection and delivery schedules, yet even so it cost the railways a lot of time, money and (not least) a great loss of reputation. Following a major re-think on BR's involvement in both bus and lorry operation, a major change was introduced with the Transport Act in 1968. After this came the transfer of the sundries network to the newly formed National Freight Corporation, and the parcels network changed to become the prospectively more effective RAIL EXPRESS PARCELS; along with this the livery changed from the earlier maroon and cream or yellow to a very modern white and blue.

SUNDRIES TRAFFIC

As we began the last chapter with a reference to the financial operation of the Express Parcels business, we should continue the theme by sub-titling this chapter 'How to lose even more millions'. This is not inappropriate because, whilst the express parcels operation may have handled the greater number of individual items, the sundries network had far bigger problems. The Sundries Fleet handled everything possible under the sun, from shoes to hats, from safety pins to wire coil, and from bicycle tyres to ladders. There was no consistent shape or size or even type of package and of course there were only minimal mechanical aids to help the staff.

The basic premise of this operation was the movement of 'less than wagon load traffic'. In simple terms this meant that small consignments would be grouped at the despatch depot into covered rail vans for the rail journey, then removed from these at the destination depot and put onto road vehicles for final delivery. This operation sounds fine in theory, but forgets one major and financially insurmountable problem, which centred on the fact that there were potentially 4,700 different destinations and it was logistically impossible to give direct links between anything but the main centres.

Above: *Places like Liverpool's Spekeland Road Sundries Depot were strictly 'off limits' to the railway enthusiast. Here we see a collection of Mechanical Horses, Scarabs and mobile cranes at work off-loading trailers for onward movement.* BR (LMR)

As a result a great deal of transhipping of goods had to take place within secondary depots to keep the number of rail movements to a minimum. At one time there was a rule that unless the rail van link between two depots could guarantee at least three tons of traffic each night, then the link would be removed and the traffic sent by an alternate route which would then of course delay the delivery.

This problem of transhipping and inherent delay was well known to the railway management in the late 1930s who, but for the outbreak of hostilities, would have resolved the issue by adopting the system of 'zones', which was eventually established after the war. In these zones one major depot (usually a railhead) acted as a distribution centre. Here, sundries traffic (for an area previously covered by a number of smaller depots) would be received and literally bulked up together to make up full loads for road vehicles to deliver directly to the customers. Previously, each individual station might have received a number of feeder rail vans from different originating depots.

Above: *This rather nice working photograph shows trailers being loaded and is typical of the way most depots would be worked. The picture also features a 3-ton Scammell Scarab (OLD 542), which was supplied new to London's Bishopsgate goods depot in February 1954, this vehicle replaced an earlier Scammell mechanical horse. The view also well illustrates the Scammell coupling gear on the trailer.* Scammell Lorries Ltd.

Below: *Parcel sorting at a busy Liverpool depot. This gives some indication of the scale of the operation, and from such a picture one can see how problems of mis-routing could arise. Add to this the fact that the rail vans (on which the goods were moved) were often delayed on their incoming journey, and you will get some idea of the poor levels of service that had to be endured by the long suffering customer.* BR LMR

The process of cutting down the number of depots handling sundries traffic continued at a slow pace during the first few years, but by the mid-1950s the depot numbers had been dramatically reduced. This idea of reducing depot numbers gave both a cost saving and a decrease in transit times, thereby potentially giving a better service and bringing more traffic onto the railways. The Modernisation Plan of 1954 gave a great spur to the closure of smaller depots, thereby (theoretically) giving the railways money to update the network. The end result was a network of large new depots, each serving an extended delivery area and giving more opportunities for direct routing of rail vans between these new centres. Each depot was planned with reception sidings for the incoming rail vans where they could be unloaded directly onto platform-level conveyors, which ran the whole length of the depot.

The parcels would be sent along the conveyor and then removed at the specific point allocated to a certain delivery route where they would be placed on a trailer. The trailers were parked at right angles to these conveyors, and once these 'stand trailers' were full they would be removed to the parking area and replaced by an empty trailer. As one of the tractors came back from a journey with an empty trailer, it would pick up a loaded trailer from the parking area and set off out again.

For traffic being despatched from the depot, a number of empty rail vans would be placed on the sidings. Each of these were given a destination label and the incoming road vehicles would 'perambulate' round the rail vans, dropping the parcels into the relevant rail vehicle until all the goods had been transferred. At this juncture it might be as well to point out that although the operation detailed above might look good in theory, in practice the levels of service were atrociously low. The first major drawback was the simple act of routing the rail vans. It was only the largest depots that could offer direct rail links between each other, with the result that a lot of en-route shunting and also the transfer of goods between rail wagons at depots was required.

One only has to look at human nature to know what to expect and of course rail vans could get lost in transit for days at a time. Furthermore, whilst shunting was taking place, there was an ever-increasing chance of damage to the goods inside the vans. Another major problem was that of paperwork, as there were no consignment notes to follow the goods through their journey. Instead a summary was made of the loading of each rail van, then another summary was made on delivering the goods, as a result 'Proof of Delivery' was hard to come by. Mis-routing and re-routing was commonplace and vast numbers of documents needed to be searched through to trace one consignment.

At the time Bill was employed in the road haulage industry, and I was in vehicle manufacturing and we can both recall the difficulties of tracing a missing parcel. Amusingly, there was also a book which some wit had written in the Parts Division of David Brown Tractors called '1,001 Ways To Lie To Customers'. Having promoted 1,000 varied and fanciful excuses for not sending out the clients goods it suggested: 'If all else fails, tell the customer you sent his parts a week ago by British Railways, make up a consignment number and tell them to ring their local station. Meanwhile, chase around production as fast as you can and get another set of spares made up.'

The book continued, "When the frustrated client rings back (after several days of chasing round the rail network) say how sorry you are and tell him you'll send out another set straight away. He will then thank you profusely and go away and tell everyone how good you are, and how poor the railways were.' Joke it may have been, but it was an almost totally irrefutable scenario, and it demonstrated to what an irredeemably low ebb our railways had sunk. A further problem was one of damage to goods both by mishandling and by ingress of water through the outer packaging. The majority of 'Sundries' vehicles were open backed and even the most conscientious of drivers would have trouble keeping his load dry throughout the year.

Despite all these problems, the sheer volume of goods being handled probably closed BR's eyes to the fact that it would have been better to have reduced the size of the operation and just retained the better paying, more profitable traffic. The fact that the Government were more than willing to throw money at the problem made it easy to make the decision to update the existing operation, rather than work out precisely what was needed for the best. Of course hindsight is a great asset, and at the time, given the intransigence of the unions and the volume of traffic involved, the railway's road transport managers certainly tried their best. Looking back on the situation that prevailed at this time (mid to late 1950s) the railway sundries delivery operation and the network trading as British Road Services Parcels (the combination of Pickfords, Hays Wharf and Carter Paterson parcels) were still the only organisations offering a full nation-wide smalls carriage service.

The existing licensing system and the ability of BR to object to the granting of new or additional licenses meant that there were no private companies such as TNT, United Carriers or Parceline offering a nation-wide smalls delivery service. The only wholly independent smalls carriers were all locally-based, operating within say a 25 mile radius. Some of these companies were, however, beginning to work together to exchange traffic and thereby offer a much wider delivery service to compete with the nationalised concerns. Of course following the de-nationalisation of BRS a number of companies commenced long distance smalls services such as London-West Riding and London-Manchester in competition with BR. Yet the Modernisation Plan for the Sundries Division went ahead with new concentration depots being built at places like, Stoke-on-Trent, Walsall and Tyneside Central amongst many others. Most of these new depots incorporated facilities for handling 'wagon load' traffic as well as the 'less than wagon load' traffic that comprised the sundries work. These new depots centralised work that had previously been spread through up to 10 or 12 smaller depots, and in theory offering improved delivery services.

Unfortunately despite the planned improvements in service many things were going wrong, and traffic declined as a result. For example from 5,500,000 tons of traffic in 1954, the figure had dropped to 3,500,000 tons in 1961. The business remained highly unprofitable with total rail/road costs of about £47,000,000 and receipts of £36,000,000 and a very bad reputation which was getting worse as time went on. There were still 1,000 stations dealing with the sundries traffic, and this caused major delays as many readers will undoubtedly recall.

Above*: One of my abiding memories of the sundry delivery work was the station at Dewsbury Wellington Road, which I recall as having platforms piled high with bales of woollen cloth at one end of the main platforms, and carpets at the other. Bill has his own visions of parcels and sundry traffic at Watford, but in either case it represented the huge diversity of goods that went by rail. Here we prove the point with this well-loaded 3-ton Scammell Scarab. Fleet number HN6016 is a Scottish region vehicle, and is hauling a consignment of carpets for export. The destinations stencilled on the hessian bags include, Beira, Bulawayo and Port Elizabeth.*

Below*: Back in Leicester once again, we see a fairly standard Commer 25-cwt integral parcels van working for the Midland Region. The photograph of OAR 399 shows that the design cosmetically owes much to the pre-war N1 model. This van, which has fleet number 1582 D displays a very nice poster promoting travel to Northern Ireland. F.Cassell.*

Above: *The Morris Commercial shown above, is the same van seen on page 11 in the company of the Scammell Scarab mechanical horse collecting traffic from Dryads in Leicester. On this occasion the Morris is seen on the express parcels service in the city, but presumably not competing for just one parcel with the slower sundries service.* F. Cassell

Below: *Still in Leicester, WRO 500 is another member of the local delivery fleet and has the BR number 2003C M. Unlike the many BMC types used on the Midland Region, this example is a Commer Q25 parcel van with a 4-cylinder engine. This type of van was exceptionally popular with BR who bought it as a chassis-cowl version, and came to be preferred over standard factory-built vans as the railways found it more satisfactory to build their own bodies. Other big users of this chassis were the makers of ice cream vans and bread delivery vehicles.* F. Cassell

The trouble was that even by this period very few depots were able to offer direct links to more than a handful of other depots, and the problems of damage and loss of goods in transit remained. The result of this situation was a study that started in 1961 and in turn led to a National Sundries Plan of 1962. The main thrust of this plan was to reduce the number of depots handling sundries traffic to just 244, so obviously closures and therefore re-routing of traffic were to be the norm for the next few years. These led to even more problems and, to some extent, the bulk of sundries traffic that stayed loyal to the railways during this period were either those traffic flows which did not require urgent delivery, or were goods from customers who felt that cheap transit rates outweighed the inconvenience.

Ironically, when management had finally got a firm grip on the situation towards the end of the 1960s, they then found that the Government were planning to hive off the Sundries Division to the road-biased National Freight Corporation as National Carriers Ltd. in 1968. On 1st January 1969 the Railways Sundries Division became part of this new corporation taking with them 10,000 road vehicles and 25,000 trailers. There were grandiose plans to spend £5 million on 6,000 new trucks and trailers, ostensibly to develop and modernise storage and distribution facilities and widen the current sundries and smalls limit up to 3-tons.

Much later in 1987 the erstwhile sundries division, now trading as National Carriers merged with Roadline (the new name for the BRS parcels service) to form Lynx express carriers. Just ten years later Lynx had a turnover of £94m with 3,200 employees and 1,500 vehicles, a far cry from the fleets in 1948. The one shining star in the sundries operation, which traded as the Contract Services Division, stayed almost intact when transferred to the NFC and much later this formed the basis of EXEL LOGISTICS, who are now one of the leading logistics suppliers in the United Kingdom and Europe. Here the policy was to offer a complete collection, warehousing, sorting, trunking and delivery operation to many manufacturers, often painting the vehicles in customers livery (just as the GWR did before the war ended). The NFC later became the National Freight Company when shares in the company were sold on the open market.

To turn now to the lorries and vans operated by the smalls/sundries division we firstly need to look back to the early 1930s. At this time the only major railway road operation still in the hands (or feet) of the horse and waggon, was town cartage. This was the delivery of cartage and 'sundry smalls' into congested towns and cities and required ultra manoeuvrable vehicles, a facility that the horses could provide. The mechanisation of this operation led to the introduction of the three-wheeled Mechanical Horse (plus associated trailers) and these vehicles became the mainstay of the sundries division upon nationalisation in 1948. Away from the congested towns a number of rigid vans made up the delivery fleet. In 1948 Scammell introduced an updated mechanical-horse named the Scarab and this again proved to be the ideal successor to its forebears. This amazing little tractor unit is also to be featured in a forthcoming **Nostalgia Road**, to complement the existing title *Mechanical Horses* written by Bill Aldridge.

Both types of 'mechanical horse' were used with an astoundingly wide variety of trailers, initially flat platform trailers, but as the customers got more sophisticated a number of different styles of van bodied trailers were introduced. Although there were two types of mechanical-horse and Scarab (3-ton and 6-ton) the majority of sundries units were of the 3-ton variety. This enabled them to operate in conjunction with both the original Karrier Cob three-wheel tractors, and the Cob's ultimate replacement the four-wheel Karrier Bantam tractor unit. In all, something like 10,000 Scammell three-wheelers came to be supplied to the railways in the period 1933-1968.

British Railways also experimented with battery-electric 'horses' often based on Crompton Parkinson designs. In addition the purchase of a number of Jen-Tugs was made. These 4-wheel articulated horses had a lower capacity than the Scammell's and were thought to be ideal for rapidly diminishing loads. Unfortunately their lightweight build (they were based on car-derived components), meant that their life span was thankfully short. In the outer delivery areas more normal four-wheeled lorries (bodied as flats or vans) were used.

The 3-ton Scarab was superseded by an updated model called the Townsman in 1964 and 1,290 of these fibre-glass cabbed tractors were ordered in 1966. Along with this substantial order 1,090 Karrier Bantam articulated tractors and 950 Bedford TK articulated tractors of 8- to 10-ton capacity were purchased for use on longer routes. This latter part of the order was probably brought about by the forthcoming relaxation on trunking by road from 1967, and partly in line with improvements brought about by the 'Sundries Plan' of 1962.

As ever the Government meddled with the plans for the service, as for instance when the 1962 Act had specifically prohibited BR from carrying freight 'throughout' by road, by 1967 this was allowed where 'it is cheaper and quicker to do!' It saw substantial improvement in the overall situation, but in effect it was far too late for any lasting benefit, and already the nimble road transport operators had seen a way into the market. One specific example I can recall was the movement of textiles between the mills of West Yorkshire and the garment makers in Greater Manchester, where firms like Ripponden & District, Hanson and United Carriers soon captured the market.

The last year of railway ownership of the sundries operation saw the introduction of the Ford D Series 'Baby Artic' as a possible successor for the Bantam. Yet, as the operation moved through the 1960s there was found to be less need for articulated units. When the system was at its peak it was vital to make use of stand trailers just to contain the traffic, and the tractor units would come back two or three times a day to exchange empty trailers for full ones. However, as the traffic levels declined and each individual delivery route increased in length and duration, it was found to be more economic to employ larger trucks, both rigid and articulated. So the era of the mechanical horse wound gently down, though they were still in gainful employment in the early 1970s on urban routes. By this time the era of BR-owned road delivery vehicles had come to its end, but it is wholly impossible to assess how much tax-payers' money had been lost in just 20 years. It is almost undoubtedly counted in tens of millions, but quite probably even more!

Above: *Fleet No. 7FD 3386 is one of the many Fordson Thames 4D 566E 3-ton platform trucks, used all over the railway network. This one featured a platform body built at Temple Mills in London.* C. Green

Below: *With the registered number BLW 166B, denoting that this was a new vehicle in 1964, this photograph shows a Karrier Bantam 3-ton tractor unit with a 5-ton box van trailer unit. It is allocated to the Southern Region (Sundries) and is painted in the Yellow Rail Freight with the twin arrow logo (in red), at Brighton in July 1964. Although it was only a few months old at the time of the picture, the tractor unit has obviously seen much accidental damage. This was not uncommon and this view illustrates a common problem with the BR road vehicle fleet during the period concerned.* Peter Love

WAGON LOAD TRAFFIC

This chapter describes the wonderful variety of road vehicles that came to be operated for the delivery of traffic that was consigned in full rail wagon loads, to the numerous stations and goods yards across the country. The traffic itself was, if possible, even more varied than that carried by the Sundries Division. Amongst the goods it handled were agricultural tractors and machinery, structural steel, bridge girders, bricks, cable drums, timber, electrical equipment, beer, explosives, glass, grain, linoleum, malt, paper, tar, cars, caravans, animals on the hoof and even complete farms (except the farm buildings). Each type of traffic was given specific carriage rates and there were written instructions for all staff on how to load these products safely on to both road and rail vehicles.

Often this traffic was handled outside in the goods yard, rather than in a cosy depot or warehouse, although there were many single-road goods sheds that had a crane mounted on the loading platform to enable heavier goods to be transhipped from open wagons. The fleet of road motors used for the delivery of these items had to be flexible enough to handle any of the traffic types mentioned above, so the trucks employed were normally the heavier rigid vehicles, rather than the lighter articulated fleets of the sundries division. This is not to say that no articulated lorries or mechanical horses were to be found in this fleet, it is just that they performed different functions.

Above: *In a busy scene at Walsall freight depot in 1962, a Dennis Horla tractor unit and trailer is seen collecting steel bars.* BR

Where the traffic flows were not regular then an articulated unit would normally be supplied from one of the larger depots to save tying up a complete rigid lorry, because a tractor unit could couple up to a range of different trailers to do a variety of work during an allocation. Because of the differing nature of the work, BR management felt that they were able to experiment with a wide variety of new ideas to attract more traffic to the railway network. As common carriers they still had to carry whatever traffic may be offered to them, but there were also some sparkling innovations in improving the handling of some of the more obscure types of freight. An example of this can be found in new containerised traffic.

The original 1928 road/rail container design had, by the early-1950s, really stood the test of time. It was available in a variety of capacities, ranging from models designed to carry frozen foods, to empty baked bean cans, and from brick containers to shock-absorbing units carrying glass or porcelain. However, the standard container had its drawbacks especially for firms who could not make up a full load, so for those customers who required a similar service for small consignments they developed the SW (small wheeled) container. Mounted on castors and capable of carrying 1-ton it was easily moved from road to rail vehicle and offered the customer peace of mind since no transhipping of goods took place.

Top Right: *This Foden short wheelbase tractor with 2 multi-wheeled semi-trailers has a London registration plate, and must have been at least 16-years old when seen with this cumbersome load of steel beams destined for the M4 Motorway near Newport in 1966.*

Centre Right: *A dedicated railhead centre was set up at Rood End in Birmingham, to cater for steel deliveries into the area as seen with this 1960 Foden KGHT5/5 loading steel bars for delivery.*

Bottom Right: *Douglas Equipment Ltd. of Cheltenham, started manufacturing commercial vehicles in 1947, and chose to specialise in the four-wheel drive field. The photo shows the rear view of a Douglas tractor owned by the Eastern Region of British Railways. S.Vickery and Bill Aldridge Collection.*

A further step in containerisation was seen with the introduction of demountable bulk or powder tanks, which were forerunners of today's ISO tankers. Another, quite brilliant concept, was the Collico Case. These collapsible alloy packing cases (which came in various sizes) were hired to a supplier, who would pack them with goods and ship them by rail to their customer, from where BR would later collect the empties and return them for re-use.

Two rather unusual operations concerned the summer agricultural shows and the movement of stage shows lock, stock and barrel. The 'Big Four', had shown great foresight by moving equipment and setting up the stands and exhibits for manufacturers and distributors at the large agricultural shows throughout the country. In BR days personnel, and a wide range of railway-owned equipment, would be seconded to this job throughout the summer months; on one occasion a total of 200 railwaymen took responsibility for the handling of 8,000 tons of show equipment. Another job was to transport theatre companies and their paraphernalia from town to town using the cartage fleet to move everything from the station to the theatre. Circuses were another such type of customer; not only did the railways move the entire entourage, they often provided the winter quarters. For example, at one time elephants were 'wintered' in the vaults below Carlisle's Citadel Station.

One of the problems in producing a book on the subject of railway lorries is that each sector of the operation could warrant a book to itself, and the wagon load traffic is no exception. On nationalisation this area of operation found itself lumbered with a very outdated fleet of lorries, many of which were heavy trucks from the early 1930s. These were still in daily use as new trucks were hard to come by, but a quick answer was to purchase war surplus lorries as an interim measure. The railways then placed orders for new vehicles with the major manufacturers, but deliveries were very slow as the Government exhortation was 'Export or Die'. Eventually new trucks did arrive, and not only from the regular suppliers, as there were also Maudslays, Sentinels and Vulcans being added to the rather eclectic selection of Crossleys and Bedfords purchased from the Government. Wherever possible the chassis had bodies put on them by the railway workshops, although these establishments were initially very busy with new wagons and carriages.

Top Left: *In an attempt to keep the long-distance freight on the rails, BR introduced new freight services such as the 'Condor'. This was an overnight door to door container service from London and Birmingham to Scotland. Unfortunately the new Metropolitan Vickers Co-Bo diesels allocated to the service were completely unreliable, but when the service was handed to more reliable locomotives, this integrated road-rail service demonstrated its true potential. This led to the introduction of new services, including the 'Speedfreight' network of container trains, which were included in the 1963 timetable following year long trials. BR-LMR*

Centre Left: *One scheme, which failed to live up to expectations, was the 'Road-railer'. This was a single axle box van which, by pivoting the axles, could be made to run on road or rails. When the trailers were connected together, they could be formed up into complete trains. The prototypes were based on an American concept, and built by Pressed Steel. Unfortunately, despite its promise, various factors worked against the concept; firstly the unladen weight was too high and they appeared unstable when running at anything above moderate speeds; secondly, the flows of traffic they were intended to carry were not altogether compatible with the routes available. BR*

Bottom Left: *Another odd scheme was the 'Bulkrane', which used an 8-wheel Foden fitted with a highly modified skip-loader body able to lift and transport 9 different types of bulk containers, two at a time, each of up to 6.25 tons capacity for the movement of lime, cement, salt, or even malt. Like the similar demountable bulk petrol tanker it was not a success, though much later the small 20 foot ISO container offered all the benefits of this system with none of its drawbacks. BR*

Purchase orders were placed with Albion, Austin/Morris, Bedford, Ford, and of course Scammell who began offering its new 'Scarab' model in 1948. The Scarabs came in two capacities, for 3- and 6-ton loads, and operated with a superb variety of trailers including drop frames, pole trailers, half-tilt vans, glass carriers and even extendible flat trailers. Whilst many of the new trucks came complete with factory-built cabs, the railway workshops were not averse to building their own versions when they had time. Some Scarabs had wooden cabs fitted to replace damaged steel cabs whilst some Albions and Austin/Morris models featured fibreglass cabs, but by the end of the 1950s virtually all new trucks came with the proper factory-built cabs.

All through this period there were regular purchases of drawbar tractors, which were used for the handling of heavy or outsize loads. The Foden marque was mostly chosen, but the Eastern Region took an altogether different tack, and in replacing its time-expired Latils it bought a small fleet of Douglas four-wheel drive and four-wheel steer tractors. From the mid-1950s the realisation that the wagon load traffic could easily be lost from the railways network, in an era of better and improving road communications, made the railway management look at ways of both finding alternative traffic and better ways of handling that which existed.

As the years went by,6 the use of wheeled and demountable road/rail bulk tanks was extended and a variety of the exciting smaller open top bulk containers were promoted further for the supply of materials to building sites. Another good scheme that should have been extended was the trunk movement of biscuits, pre-loaded in delivery drop order at the factory, into special 3-ton containers/van bodies owned by McVitie & Price. The containers were loaded at the Edinburgh factory and trunked by rail to Newcastle for transfer onto special lorries, which carried out the final delivery to the retail outlets.

One operation that to some extent is still with us today was the total separation of certain categories of freight into their own terminals. Apart from coal concentration depots, the first major scheme of freight concentration was with steel products. Special 'steel only' freight trains operated to these depots, which were located in important centres like the Black Country, and offered a next day delivery on behalf of the steel producers in places like Scotland, Wales, Scunthorpe and Sheffield.

The heyday of the 'less than wagon load' operation was from the inter-war period up till the late-1950s, but by this time the difficulty of profitably and making up train loads of individual wagons to varied destinations was beginning to rear its ugly head. The costs of the operation were beginning to outweigh the benefits, in fact it was exactly the same problem as found with the sundries network. The gradual loss of remote goods stations was followed by more closures across the country leading to a haemorrhage of traffic as more and more customers were forced to put their traffic on the road.

Although Dr. Beeching had many faults in his general prognosis for the recovery of the railway, the loss of wagon load traffic was correctly identified as an existing and ongoing problem. Given that the railways could not offer an economic 'throughout by road' service, this operation was already doomed, but Beeching rapidly hastened the end by accelerating the closure of depots making it very hard for any but the most dedicated customers to remain loyal to the railways.

Top Right: A *Scammell 3-ton Mechanical Horse with an extendible platform trailer at Grimsby. This vehicle, HXW 477 was purchased by the LNER as a replacement for a Karrier Cob Junior on 1st August 1947, interestingly it was itself sold on 2nd February 1962, for just £4.* Colin Green Collection.

Centre Right: *This pair of Eastern Region Scammell Scarabs shows the difference between the standard steel (Willenhall) cab fitted to the majority of Scammell tractor units as displayed on LUV 21, and one of the wooden cabs built at BR's Temple Mills works on KXY 186. Both Scarabs dated from 1950; but of these KXY 186 remained in service until 1964, whereas LUV 21 lasted until July 1965.* H.S. Transport Collection

Bottom Right: *This Scarab (MLE 449), seen working with a glass float trailer in London in the mid-1950s. was new in December 1951, and numbered HK 6611. The vehicle in the background appears to be a post-war Bedford KV.* HUB Publishing

To give an idea of the variety of a railway driver's life and the jobs that were carried out during the hey-day of this operation, we recall some of the work done by Sydney Bourne from Stoke on Trent who joined the LMS in 1946 and became a 'district driver' in the town in 1951. The cartage delivery area then was from Bollington (Cheshire) in the north, and going as far south as Leek in Staffordshire, and then west to Malpas near to the Shropshire border.

A total of 11 men were employed as relief drivers in this team, and although they moved around the area as work demanded, they might stay at one depot for up to three months at a time whilst campaigns were taking place. At one time there were 20,000 tons of steel to move (on vehicles with a maximum capacity of 6-tons!) in the form of steel pipe for the water pipeline from Rudyard Lake (near Leek), and it was all to be moved by rail and cartage vehicles. The Stoke to Stafford trunk operation was run by a 1949 Karrier Bantam articulated lorry.

Whilst the vehicles driven by Mr. Bourne included the older 'Mechanical Horses', Scarabs and Bantams, and even bonneted Albions dating from the early-1930s; but there were also Morris Commercials with the Saurer based engine (which would run backwards at times) as well as modern Bedford TKs. These latter vehicles came new with factory-built platform bodies, but they were very soon changed for harder wearing BR bodies. However, before a man was able to drive a different vehicle to his usual one, he had to be tested on that particular type in order to ensure he was both familiar with it and capable of driving it. In this particular operation, it is evident that a great degree of flexibility was needed for Mr. Bourne recalls that management at the new Stoke sundries depot worked on the basis of what was best for the customer, rather than worry about strict demarcation between parcels-sundries-cartage. At times, to keep things moving, even the maintenance department's Fordson E83W van was pressed into delivery service.

But very soon it would all come to an end, and as we have already seen, the 1968 Transport Act led to changes in the Rail Express Parcels operation, and the hand-over of the sundries business to the NFC; however, this same massive retraction in BR road vehicle operation led to the virtual abandonment of the 'wagon load' business and (to all intents and purposes) its traffic was handed over to private road hauliers.

Top Left: *This BMC 501 articulated tractor (ULY 651) is in service with the Western Region at Llantwit Major station in 1965, where it is being loaded with steel girders by two BR-owned Shelvoke & Drewry Freightlifters working together.* S.Vickery

Centre Left: *A more modern tractor unit is seen with this 1964 model Bedford TK, in the sand coloured Railfreight livery at the Aberthaw power station in Wales. It has fleet number 8556D W.* S.Vickery

Bottom Left: *A brand new Bedford TK tractor unit showing the Scammell automatic coupling is seen in 1967. This was NMP 492E, fleet No. BVA1492 E, which is now sporting the new BR yellow livery with the red double arrow logo.* BR ER

Above: *Colour pictures of British Railways road vehicles are few and far between, and despite constantly seeking images since the first edition of the book was published in 1997, few have come to light. However, the images in this new colour centre section are an essential improvement over the first edition, in that they will help readers (especially model-makers) visualise how the black and white images would have looked in real life. Although this picture graced the front cover of the first edition of this book, its move to the centre page section does not in any way detract from the timeless quality of the preserved station forecourt at Oxenhope. This Scammell Scarab is based at the Keighley and Worth Valley Railway, but is a regular attender at events organised by the Mechanical Horse Club. Originally allocated to the North Eastern Region, NDN 753 carries a York registration plate.* Alan Earnshaw

Above: *With a Brighton registration plate, 884 FUF is a real trip down Nostalgia Road for me personally, as my summer holidays in the 1950s were spent at my Aunt Marion's newsagency in this south coast resort. We always arrived by rail, and then travelled around the district by Southdown bus, and so the 'UF' plate was well known to me. However, this Fordson E83W van was originally registered OAR 223 and dates from 1951. It has been very well restored and is seen here at Horsted Keynes Station in December 2000.* Jeff College

Left: *The railways always had a number of heavy haulage tractors, but even monochrome pictures of these beasts are hard to find. This image of a Foden ballast tractor at Shrewsbury, fleet number 480W, is therefore well worthy of inclusion in this colour section. Note the ladder carelessly laying against the rear end, and the way in which the spare wheel is carried behind the cab.*

Above: *This stunning picture is worth a thousand words, as it shows a Bedford HA van in an experimental Express Parcels livery at Hitchin in 1966. It also makes revenge a little sweeter, as I was once taken to task by another railway historian who criticised an article I wrote on experimental road vehicle liveries and stated that BR never had powder blue vehicles. Well what can't speak can't lie, but apart from that this is a view that just had to be included. The Royal Mail Morris Commercial and the Carmine and Cream Bedford CA Crew Bus just add to the atmosphere. Vauxhall Motors*

Right: *Although a picture of rather poor quality, this view of Scammell Scarab NVY 344 taken at Leeds in June 1964 is highly representative of the railway road vehicle fleet at that time. With the fleet number HN 6178N, the 3-ton Mechanical Horse is paired to covered trailer CT31407. It is pictured in company with parcel vans on Fordson, Morris and Karrier chassis.*

Above: *In service with the Signalling & Telegraph department of British Railways at Luton, this Bedford HA Van was actually photographed whilst on trial from local vehicle manufacturers, Vauxhall Motors. Careful inspection will reveal that KYM 8P does not carry any BR fleet numbers. After this trial it was used by the Express Parcels operation at Welwyn Garden City. The blue DMU in the background is M51881 a Derby-built Class 115 Motor Brake Second (4-sub).* Vauxhall Motors

Left: *Seen at Norwich as late as 14th July 1973, this 1965-registered Morris FG is part of the BR Road Vehicle operation that survived the 1968 disposals. Like the Commer Walk-Thru van behind it, it is part of the Rail Express Parcels fleet. Pictured in a yellow, blue and white livery DYF 78C is typical of many of the vans in this fleet during the early 1970s. Its drab appearance and less than well-cared-for state reflects the low-ebb to which railway road vehicle operation had sunk by this time.* R. Taylor

THE ROAD VEHICLE FLEET 1948-1954

When the Government took on responsibility for the nation's transport systems on 1st January 1948, it was greatly assisted by the Big Four railway companies. In fact, a period of co-operation had begun during the war and continued to nationalisation, especially during the last quarter of 1947. This co-operation was seen in all areas of activity, but (arguably) most of all in the road vehicle operations of the railway companies, for in this area alone the private companies had already come to a logical traffic sharing and vehicle operating scheme in many parts of the country over a decade earlier. One such area of co-operation had been seen during the grave winter conditions of 1946-7, when pooled traffic arrangements were the norm as a Winter Transport Executive Committee directed the nation's transport arrangements. As a consequence of the great difficulties during the early part of 1947, a similar arrangement was set up in 1948-9 in an attempt to avert a similar crisis on the nation's railways and canals.

Above: *A Scottish Region Jensen Jen-Tug petrol tractor and trailer (HGE 283), was oddly given a coupling that was totally incompatible with Scammell trailers.* BR-ScR

These seasonal arrangements encouraged the transfer of certain traffic types either onto or away from road haulage, but it was then found impossible to retreat from these measures when the winter of 1948-9 turned out to be exceptionally mild. In its annual report for its first year the BTC stated 'the Commission cannot escape the conclusion that this factor is one of the contributory causes of the unsatisfactory financial results of railway operation during 1948.'

Nevertheless, throughout that first year the BTC strove towards its given policy of establishing an integrated operation of inland transport, ports and airports. Yet, the continuing growth in the numbers of road vehicles being licensed and the increasing trend for businesses to take out their own operators 'C' license was having its effect on British Railways and its associated road vehicle fleet.

By December 1948 the number of vehicles carrying these 'C' licenses had increased by 103,365 over the previous year's figures and reached an all-time high of 590,516. This represented a monthly increase of around 8,614 and this continued the worrying trend of 1946 and 1947; prior to this it should be stated that the pre-war monthly increase in 'C' licences was around the 200 mark. Although most of the vehicles so licenced were 30-cwt or below, it is plain that this increase was vitally affecting the BTC's policy of planning and fixing charges, thus undermining the proposals for a completely integrated transport policy. It certainly had a detrimental effect on the road collection and delivery service provided by British Railways in its first year, and in its annual report the BTC stated: 'The receipts and expenditure of these services, which consist almost entirely of Collection and Delivery Services directly connected with rail shipment are set out.... The loss shown is a normal feature of these operations, which are regarded as an ancillary service rather than a separate trading activity.

The receipts at £8.4 million for collection and delivery are some 18 percent above the receipts for 1947. This reflects mainly the increase in charges sanctioned in October 1947. Of the working expenses, vehicle license duties remained virtually unchanged at £0.4m; wages of drivers and attendants rose only from £6.2m to £6.7m, and amounts paid for hired cartage actually fell to £1.6m from £1.9m. The results reflect the substantial reduction of horse-drawn cartage in favour of the so-called Mechanical Horse and other steps towards a quicker cheaper operation were also taken during the year.'

Below: *This picture shows a side valve engine being carefully lifted out of a Scarab prior to its general overhaul; it also clearly shows the centrally-mounted radiator. Standardisation of vehicle types and larger maintenance depots were one of the successes of the BR road fleet operation, and operatives (both drivers and mechanics) became well accustomed to their steeds.* BR LMR

At the end of 1948 the railway road fleet comprised of 11,329 motor vehicles, 735 cars and 265 special vehicles (eg. cranes, agricultural tractors and crawler tractors). This was a wide and varied fleet with very little form of central control, although early in 1948 the BTC did go some way to addressing this problem with its introduction of 'Statistical Control'. In application this led to the examination of outstanding problems such as the high costs of London cartage, exclusion of hiring in vehicles, how to obtain more intensive use of the Executive's own vehicles, experimental work with low load capacity electric vehicles, and above all the withdrawal of the horse-drawn fleet.

There was still a stud of 7,404 horses, most of which had two or three carts. Yet the statistics of these resources showed reasons for growing concern, especially in view of the escalating costs of fodder and veterinary care that were being experienced at a time when animal welfare regulations were demanding a reduction in the working conditions for beasts of burden. Thereafter the horse stud, although declining in numbers, was treated as an entirely separate operation which transcended regional boundaries.

An attempt was also made to standardise the types in the road motor fleet, in anticipation of annual renewal programmes. The primary objectives were:- increased efficiency, driver operating knowledge, economy of maintenance and a reduction of the multiplicity of spare parts that had to be stocked. A new safety programme was instituted and driver training programmes 'beefed up'. Maintenance arrangements were centralised where possible and the construction of an improved repair shop was authorised for the Western Region at Gloucester. On Teesside, central repair arrangements were instituted at Stockton-on-Tees. Meanwhile the design department at Derby drew up plans for a 'standard' body for the various chassis that were on order. Even so, the total deficit for the year was a staggering £3,947,810.

During 1949 receipts for express parcels traffic were up by 2% over the 1948 figures, with a significant increase being noted from the textile industries of West Yorkshire and the East Midlands. It was a similar trend with newspapers and periodicals, as a relaxation in the paper ration allowed the size of the publications to be increased.

Unfortunately, the flow of agricultural traffic, notably milk, fruit, flowers and vegetables diminished significantly during what turned out to be a dry summer. All of this had an effect on road haulage services, as did the increasing number of branch line and station closures that came about during 1949. In strict terms this affected a considerable number of cartage services, and as a result 100 vehicle routes were withdrawn and 700 horses were dispensed with. Older vehicles were scrapped, others were used at new locations where the services of cartage agents were terminated, often with only minimal notice.

Interestingly, despite the rising cost of materials, the standardisation which had commenced the previous year had already begun to show savings, especially among the newer Scarabs which were being ordered in significant quantities. The Scarab, incidentally, had just been put into full production having been found to fully justify its introduction, meanwhile an increase in the number of small electric vehicles was also noted, and at first these showed remarkable operating success.

Above: *In the post-war years, BR continued the purchasing policy of its constituents, several of whom had been extremely loyal to the Thornycroft range. The backbone of this range was mainly the Sturdy, Trusty and the Nippy models. Here, a Shelvoke & Drewry Freightlifter is seen loading a BD container onto the step-frame trailer of a late-1940s Thornycroft Nippy in service with the Western Region. My co-author Bill Aldridge can talk about this subject with some authority having part restored a similar Nippy tractor.* BR WR

Below: *Safe driving and best kept vehicle competitions were regular features in fleet operations in the 1950s. Here we see driver Chadburn of Burton-on-Trent receiving an award for the best kept vehicle (JJH 535) a Scammell 3-ton MH. Note the change in vehicle livery from the same vehicle pictured the previous year and shown on page 10.* Bill Aldridge Collection

Above: *By the end of 1949 there was a stock of 12,972 motor vehicles, 17,823 trailers and 177 cars; these figures include 754 non-revenue earning vehicles. The horse stud continued to decline, with numbers reducing to 6,095. The vehicles that were retained, were nearly all re-painted in the Carmine and Cream livery by the end of 1953; an example of this livery is this (non-revenue) Thornycroft Nippy, fitted with a Hampshire Car Bodies cab which was employed in the Western Region's Signal & Telegraph department at Teignmouth, Devon.* BR WR

Below: *This BR diesel-engined Fordson Thames bus, was used for the transportation of railway maintenance workers, and was what we would now call a PW crew bus. The handsome, but never-the-less very angular body probably had a drag factor slightly less than an average council house.* Bill Aldridge

These measures combined to give savings of 0.4d per mile, or a total of £23,000 on the annual maintenance costs, but this widely quoted figure of the day took no account of the fact that a very high percentage of the fleet were now relatively new vehicles, and thus required significantly less maintenance than the 20-year old lorries that they had replaced. Meanwhile, the new WR lorry workshops in Gloucester opened on 21st November. During the year BR took delivery of 1,104 motor vehicles, 1,973 trailers and an increasing number of cars.

By 1950 the BTC and its Railway Executive had apparently settled down into a period of relative stability, and at last a number of the policies were beginning to produce dividends, the only point of regret was the announcement of his intended retirement by Sir Eustace Missenden; his successor being John Elliot from the London Midland Region. Other major changes saw the transfer of the railway-owned docks and canals to the Docks & Inland Waterways Executive, whilst jointly operated electric lines in the London area were handed over to the London Transport Executive.

The process of closing unremunerative lines continued apace, and 145 passenger route miles went with the loss of 31 stations. Of these route miles 48.5 were closed completely, along with 89.75 route miles on freight-only lines. This represented an alleged saving of £234,000, yet compared with £2.8 million losses incurred by the road delivery and collection service, this was a mere flea-bite. In actual fact, the year showed a £900,000 saving on the losses of the previous year, but the gross receipts were just £9,500,000 for the entire road service. This was identical to the £900,000 difference on the £8,600,000 receipts of 1949, but when we take into consideration that the railways had increased their prices significantly on 15th May 1950, this should have sounded the alarm bells ringing—the road haulage service was not simply 'holding its own' as one report claimed, it was actually slipping further and further into the red. The year had seen an increase in the price of petrol and stores to the tune of £400,000, and a £100,000 increase in maintenance charges. The amount of freight collected and delivered was 32,009,000 tons, whilst 154,850,000 million parcels were handled, and both figures were an increase on the 1949 totals, but was it profitably undertaken? Probably not, but as the railway took delivery of 1,748 new motor vehicles, 2,618 trailers and 30 motor cars, the annual report stated: 'The considerable progress made in cartage mechanisation resulted in economy and greater efficiency, particularly at some of the large London depots. During the year the mechanised strength increased by 878 motors and 2,373 trailers, the additional vehicles being employed mainly in the replacement of horses.'

As of 31st December 1950 the stock of vehicles consisted of 13,858 motors, 20,196 trailers, 688 private cars and 96 motor cycles. In addition there were 797 road vehicles employed in departmental duties. In spite of further increases in the price of materials and spares, the cost of repairs fell by approximately 0.35d a mile, following a saving of 0.4d a mile in 1949. The improvement was obtained from the progress made in the introduction of standard inspection and overhaul intervals, the standardisation of vehicle types within specific areas and the elimination of very old vehicles from the fleet.

In 1950 some 30,000 vehicles were overhauled and about 68,000 inspections or running repairs were made. The average number of motors out of service for repair was equal to 6.7% of the total stock and the requirements of the operating department were fully met.' It all seemed very positive, and there were some areas that demonstrated very clear progress; safety and training being the most evident, and in some districts a joint staff training plan was set up with BRS personnel.

In Scotland a reorganisation of the road fleet meant that new maintenance depots were established at Aberdeen, Edinburgh and Glasgow, with running depots at Ayr, Dumfries and Jedburgh. Experiments with electric lorries and vans continued, so 136 of these were taken into stock and allocated to 21 city centre depots, but the Railway Executive was still not yet sure of their long term benefit. The co-operation between BR and BRS that was evident in training and safety was also obvious in other forms of integration, as the two began to work toward a common goal. This was demonstrated, as for example in Bristol, where BR lorries were overhauled at the BRS workshops and in rural Scotland, where BR took over collection and delivery duties for BRS who forwarded large consignments of goods by rail for BR to deliver to the villages, crofts and farms north of the Border. Meanwhile the horse fleet went on shrinking, and at the end of the year it was down to 4,754 and yet this season the carmen managed to win 317 awards and 118 commendations at various county or country shows.

The year 1951 was marred by a serious number of staff shortages on BR, with key personnel in all areas and departments being in short supply. As a consequence, the losses in freight traffic capacity were quite pronounced, as staff were shifted to ensure that passenger services received priority. Therefore the BTC decided that the Road Haulage Executive should deal with this shortfall in capacity, and make available road vehicles from its fleet to carry certain types of traffic throughout. As a consequence BRS had to deal with unusually heavy traffic in small consignments, at a time when it was least able to do so efficiently.

The problem of severe weather in certain parts of the country at the start of the year compounded an already difficult situation. It was one which neither BR or BRS could adequately resolve and in the first quarter of 1951 there was a substantial increase in the number of firms applying for their own 'C' licence. Yet the traffic still being handled in freight and parcels had a staggering value of £31,310,000, despite the 16.6% rise in charges that had been introduced on 15th May 1951. This served to disguise the fact that, in real terms, traffic was actually beginning to 'vanish' at an alarming rate, for the number of customers using the railway had diminished by a frightening 23.2% on 1948 totals.

This situation was, in many ways, disguised by the fact that traffic was being buoyed up by 'faithful' customers who were sending even greater amounts of goods as the relaxation in war-time restrictions were now coming to an end. The road collection and delivery work seemed to be holding steady with only a very slight decrease (1.5% goods traffic and 4.5% parcels traffic), so the expansion programme continued with 1,125 motor vehicles, and 1,477 trailers being added to the fleet. This made a total of 14,381 motor vehicles and 121,644 trailers (an actual increase of 425 and 1,448 respectively) by the end of the year.

Above: *This Midland Region 6-ton Scarab (LAR 292) is seen when new, probably in the early 1950s. With the fleet number 3106 G and complete with a drop-sided trailer for use on goods traffic, it is seen at Scammell's Watford factory on acceptance trials. Observant readers will discern that there is a distinct similarity between the cab on the Scarab and that used on the Bedford O Type lorry. In fact both sets of cab panels were made by the Willenhall Motor & Radiator Company, but the workers at Scammell had quite a tricky job in getting the doors to fit their narrower model. Scammell Lorries Ltd.*

Below: *Here is a late example of the Austin K4 Series I, pictured at a rural location, which we believe to be in Somerset. Although introduced in 1939, it did not enter serious productions until the war had ended. Like its main competitor, the Bedford O-Type, it featured a 6-cylinder petrol engine. Bill Aldridge Collection*

Above: *The staff shortages in the early 1950s created havoc on Britain's public transport system. and it became apparent that a large number of personal injuries were being reported by railwaymen. The majority of these were directly associated with men trying to handle loads that were far too heavy for just one person. As a consequence the BR Board decided to implement a staff training programme in safe-handling techniques. Shown here is a demonstration presenting the correct and safe way to unload barrels and drums from a 3-ton flat-bed trailer M5404! This picture is just one of a series of safety photos taken at St. Albans City Station in the early 1950s.* Colin Green

Below: *A nice demonstration of even loading is seen at Pyle Goods Yard, near Bridgend in 1952, as a Scammell 6-ton MH is loaded with Government 'Buffer Stores'. The neatly stacked boxes on the flat-bed trailer behind FYU 16 (Fleet No.6294) make an interesting contrast with some of the more precarious loads pictured elsewhere in this book.* S.Vickery

Mechanisation of handling was speeded up during 1951, with 80 stations (including most London depots) becoming fully equipped by the end of the year, whilst progress was under way at 58 more locations. Elimination of overlapping cartage services was finally brought to an end, or so it was claimed, and this produced operating economies of £33,000 per annum. By August, the first stage of a scheme to improve inter-London station cartage had been completed, and this resulted in savings of a further £20,000. Driver training and safety programmes had continued throughout the year, and a new driver training school was opened on the Southern Region. A significant traffic during the summer was the Festival of Britain, which ran from 3rd May to 30th September; special cartage facilities were introduced in connection with this event, and 576 extra vehicles were drafted in for this work, including 438 new vehicles. As for the horse stud, it was down to 3,294 by the year end.

The report for 1952 was a significant one, if for no other reason, than it showed a big reversal of transport policies in Britain, which came about as a result of the change of Government the previous autumn. It was the fifth year of the British Transport Commission's existence, and it was in so many ways only then that the potential of an integrated transport system was beginning to show its real worth. The acquisition of long distance haulage undertakings had finally been completed in the middle of 1951, and plans had now been set in place for a national integrated road/rail service. Joint engineering and maintenance depots had been established, with BR and BRS road vehicles sharing the same garages, whilst long distance feeder services had been planned.

More importantly, co-operation with the various trade unions had been secured regarding the transfer of staff, working arrangements, and demarcation issues, but only after very long and protracted negotiations. With the central control of certain essential matters, the management of this integrated transport system was being sharpened up by the devolution of authority down to the regions.

Yet, the greatest achievement of all was the development work that was just starting to be done under a single commercial management — it would take far more than a book of just 52-pages to fully outline the argument why this integration could have worked, but a detailed study of the circumstances will reveal the facts to those who wish to examine the issue for themselves.

However, the General Election of October 1951 was to put an end to all the grand plans, and on 8th May 1952 a White Paper was issued to forecast legislation that the new Government intended to introduce. Again it is a very complex document, but basically its main premise was that it would oblige the BTC to decentralise the railway management and dispose of their road haulage undertakings. The BTC pointed out to the new Minister of Transport that these proposals would have gravely disturbing effects, but whilst the Government listened to the BTC's objections they made it abundantly clear that they would proceed with their de-nationalisation plans whatever the cost might be in terms of service, staff morale or pounds shillings and pence. Yet, whilst the de-nationalisation of the road transport business operated by BRS did not outwardly affect the railway road vehicle fleet, it was (so to speak) the first nail in the coffin!

A telling paragraph in the BTC annual report for 1952 emphasises this saying: 'The costing of selected freight traffic made further progress during the year, but in view of the proposals contained in the Transport Bill, the study of comparative costs as a basis for the production of a freight charging scheme for both road and rail was not given a high priority. Considerable studies were made, however, of the economies of the traffics in parcels and small consignments, and these confirm the proposition that for such traffics the unit of cost is the package rather than the consignment and that distance is a much less important factor than weight, since the cost of handling, cartage and documentation far outweighs the cost of the trunk haul, particularly where traffic is rail-borne for the longer distances.'

It then concluded this thought by the all important summary, 'It seems likely that the parcels and 'smalls' traffic are no longer properly remunerative.' Yet in the size and complexity of a road/rail operation which, in 1952, saw an income of £286,541,000 in general freight, parcels and GPO traffic, and £26,472,000 for express parcels, the real underlying trends were not readily apparent. Whilst ever an integrated transport system was in place, the losses and unprofitable traffic could be buoyed up by more viable business at least until such time as the proposed new charging schemes could be introduced. However, with de-nationalisation, the profitable parts of the haulage business would be picked off by the independent sector who could pick and choose the traffics they wanted, leaving the railways and the reduced BRS fleet to carry what was left - namely all the unprofitable stuff!

During 1952, the improvement and mechanisation of the railway delivery fleet continued apace, and no less than 1,328 motor vehicles and 1,400 new trailers were put into service. The horse stud declined to 2,179 and 4,000 horse-drawn vehicles were put up for disposal. The Manchester horse-feed mill was closed, and plans were outlined for similar closures at the mills that the railways owned at Didcot and Portobello. Complete mechanisation of cartage was achieved at 60 stations with 40 more in the process of conversion at the end of the year. Collection and delivery horses had dropped to less than 100 in London, many going when the Marylebone goods depot converted to handling parcels traffic only. A similar plan was announced for King's Cross, and parcel concentration plans were put in place for introduction at Finsbury Park and five other stations, whilst suburban parcel traffic in the southern part of greater London was achieved with a new depot at Richmond.

The Marylebone conversion alone ended a traffic of 13,000 cross-city parcels a day, as traffic formerly handled at Euston and St. Pancras was centralised at the new parcels depot. Meanwhile, miscellaneous freight traffic was transferred from Acton to Park Royal, and this coincided with the closure of the goods parcels depots at Aldersgate and Eastcastle Street. All of this had the added advantage of speeding up traffic through the various junction marshalling areas around London, and simultaneously brought to an end around 1,200 shunting trip workings each day. Other special traffics handled in the year were a considerable number of flowers that were moved in connection with the funeral of King George VI, and a bumper crop of potatoes which were handled as wagon load freight in the potato-growing areas of Britain.

Above: *Another variation of the type of trailer used by BR is seen on this Derby-based unit M5801. This GT3 trailer has been built with a high headboard for the transportation of light but bulky loads. Commonly employed in areas producing textiles, the trailer is fitted with 7.50 x 20 tyres. Conversely, the tractor unit JJH 358 (Fleet No.2644G) is provided with 8.25 x 10 tyres. Note the heavy scarring on the bodywork of the tractor, a typical problem for many BR vehicles.* Bill Aldridge Collection

Below: *The firm of Sentinel were still involved with the manufacture of steam lorries until as late as 1938 for the British market, and their export models continued until the end of the 1940s. As a result their involvement with diesel lorries came at a very late stage when compared with their contemporaries. The vehicle pictured here is a 4/4 DV model, registered number OYL 463 (Fleet No.1345 S) working on the Southern Region with a drawbar trailer. It is seen here taking insulated meat containers through South London.* A. Ingram

Top Left: *This relatively rare Douglas 4 x 4 tractor, was one of a small number used by the Eastern Region. Using a two-stroke Rootes engine, these versatile trucks also featured four-wheel steering. For those not from an agricultural background, the 'strange-looking' item on the trailer is a forage harvester.* A. Ingram Collection

Centre Left: *As mentioned elsewhere in the text of this book, the railways found good profits in the transportation of equipment to and from the various county agricultural shows and the big agricultural events. Here a Bedford OSS, KXU 471 (fleet no. D8360) is leading a step-frame trailer T88948, with a Fahr combine for the Windsor Show in 1954.* S. Vickery.

Bottom Left: *Again at Windsor in 1954, step-frame trailer T88948W is seen at work, this time coupled to a Bedford OSS, registered KXU 546. It is pictured here delivering a fuel storage tank* S. Vickery

As 1953 came to its end, the BTC announced that an overall net surplus of £4.2 million had been earned after meeting central charges and other loans which had to be repaid on the gross profit of £59,400,000. It was in fact the first year that such a profit had been made, and this was achieved on the back of the integrated transport policy, but as this was now being rapidly fragmented it was to be the last! On 6th May the Transport Act 1953 received Royal Assent, and within two weeks the Road Haulage Disposal Board was established! The significance of this event was not missed by those in the industry, but it was lost on the rest of the nation who were celebrating something of much greater importance - the arrival of a new Queen.

On 2nd June 1953 the railways were exceptionally busy, as 1,338 special trains carried 1,043,649 passengers to London to watch the Coronation of Queen Elizabeth, in addition to the scheduled passenger services that were packed to capacity. The express parcels fleet were heavily involved in the operation, carrying in excess of 2 million pieces of passengers luggage sent in advance. To handle this traffic, 234 extra vans were drafted into London from the home counties. Yet despite the apparent up-turn in this new brave land, many legacies bestowed by the war years were still impacting on Britain's transport infrastructure.

In the year the Queen was crowned at Westminster Abbey, her Government authorised the BTC to spend £58,000,000 on capital improvement to new rolling stock, ships, vehicles, plant and equipment, and £10,000,000 on land. Yet of this vast sum, only £32,000,000 was actually spent on development, the other £36,000,000 was merely used to replace life-expired or prematurely worn-out capital equipment. Simultaneous with this however, was the continual shrinkage of the railway network, and few may realise just how much of the railway had been closed before Dr. Richard Beeching ever began to wield his vicious axe! For instance in 1953 alone 29 passenger, 9 freight and 15 'passenger & freight' stations had been closed along with 241 railway route miles. Since 1948 this meant that, in total, no less than 225 passenger, 84 freight and 62 'passenger & freight' stations had been sacrificed along with 1,778 route miles.

This factor, coupled with the diminishing traffic and the existance of newly formed long-distance road haulage companies, was to have a real bearing on the railway road vehicle service. Even so £2.2 million was spent on new road vehicles, with no less than 1,793 motors, and 2,945 trailers being purchased as the horse-stud dropped to just 1,221. By the end of 1954 BR's net receipts had declined from £31.5 million to just £16,600,239, with the main cause for this being attributed to higher wage costs and a strike by footplate staff on the Western Region in May.

Although this strike only caused losses of around the £700,000 mark, its long term effects were noticeable in the 'smalls' and express parcels traffics. Overall the road services arm of BR showed a deficit of £1,801.560 in 1954, and coupled with the losses made in 1953 this was now approaching a figure of £4 million. There was little chance of any recovery as the gross receipts were £12.2 million, but working expenses stood around £14 million, and this did not take into account the capital charge for new equipment nor depreciation on existing stock.

In 1953 the BRS fleet had handled 29,899,000 tons of freight, but as 1954 came to an end it was recorded that the figure had shrunk to 28,493,000 although the number of parcels handled had increased by five million to 159,651,000. Much worse was to follow in 1955, for this was the year when the Road Haulage Disposal Board announced it had disposed of the majority of the fleet. Yet, a small part of BRS had been left intact, as the Act had already made provision for some vehicles to be retained - in the event, a total of 2,341 lorries and vans.

In addition to this it was found impossible to get a buyer for the meat delivery vehicles, a fleet of 498 trucks, and some other items of specialised equipment. In the event, a total of 7,750 vehicles were retained by BRS in addition to those previously authorised, but by the end of 1955 a total of 46,024 BRS vehicles had been sold off - each of them another nail in the coffin of the nationalised railways. The railway's own fleet of road vehicles continued to lose money, but not as significantly as they had done the two preceding years.

Top Right: *Here we have a member of the Western Region fleet, which has the reporting number 5222 W. This is a Dennis Pax drop-side lorry (LLX 44) and it is seen in a Swindon works photo in February 1951.* BR-WR

Centre Right: *Fortunately, despite the apparent severity of this mishap, no-one was seriously hurt and the truck driver can be seen in the background. In this instance the ropes holding these steel water pipes do not look to have had much effect in preventing serious damage to this Scottish Region wagon EN 8009SC, an ex-LNER Commer Q25 Superpoise HGH 59 of 1945 vintage.* C. Green, Bill Aldridge Collection

Bottom Right: *Loading containers onto a brace of 6-ton Scammell Scarabs at Leigh, for transfer to the BICC works in that Lancashire town. The Scarab in BICC livery with its local issue registration plate is of 1953 vintage, while British Railways own example is a 1957 model.* British Insulated Callendar Co.

During The Suez Crisis

If there can ever be said to be a clear turning point in transport history, particularly in the road-*v*-rail debate, then it would certainly be during the middle of the 1950s. As this period primarily influenced events on the whole British transport scene, and specifically led to the Conservative Government's decision to appoint separate reports into the future of our road and rail network, and in turn these obviously affected the whole road vehicle operation of British Railways.

Strange to say, it was not even an event which began here in Britain that started it, for it began with the Middle-East problem and the Suez Crisis of 1955-6. For most of us Suez is an unknown quantity, as the true facts surrounding the events that autumn were largely kept from the British public, but the seeds of Arab revolt were first sown in 1951, when Iran claimed her oil-fields and eventually nationalised them. It was an event that did not go unnoticed by her neighbours, especially Egypt which was demonstrating a strong display of nationalism and anti-British sentiment.

Top Left: *A Pagefield Cruiser mobile crane unloads a BD container (BD6600B) at the new Marylebone goods depot, from an Austin WF series WRO 771 (5372 BGO M) with a Scammell articulated 6-ton trailer (M6268).* BR LMR

Top Right: *An example of how many BR lorries were loaded back in the 1950s, particularly those employed on sundries traffic. Simply stack the load on a flat-bed trailer and then cover same with a tarpaulin and sheet it down, as shown in Liverpool with Scarab 3268G M (LAR 502).* Bill Aldridge Collection

Centre Right: *This photograph at Fairford is fairly representative of a country station operation during the 1950s. A small depot would often cover a wide area, and have to operate both country lorry duties and express parcels services. Rather than having two vehicles, the railways would employ a vehicle with a van front and a canvas back end as seen here. Few photographs of this type of vehicle have survived in the official archive, and the authors would be delighted to hear from readers with better illustrations.*

Bottom Right: *The biggest development came in containerisation, which was seen as both the ideal answer to, and complimentary with, road-haulage as our picture above shows. Here a Vulcan 6-ton lorry is seen with an A type container outside a London warehouse. A demand was evident from traders, particularly in 1957, for the small-wheeled containers carrying up to 1-ton in capacity.* BR-WR

The situation got worse after Churchill resigned as Prime Minister in April 1955, but the greatest problem facing Britain at this time was a 17-day long railway strike, which was estimated to have cost the country £12m. This came at a time when the country could ill-afford it because our gold/dollar reserves were shrinking by approximately $100m per month. On 26th October 1956 the Chancellor, Rab Butler, announced a mini-budget, that was to result in a whole range of spending cuts, including a postponement of long-term investment plans for the railways, electricity and gas industries.

Unfortunately things in the Middle-East were deteriorating as well, and an ill-judged Anglo-French military invasion of Egypt led to the Suez Canal being blocked (and thus rendered useless) in November. Several pumping stations on the Iraq-Lebanon Oil Pipe-line were also destroyed, and Britain's 'short-cut' to the Gulf oil-fields was completely blocked. With shipping destined to thereafter take a long journey round the Cape, oil supplies to Britain were strangled and in due course petrol rationing was introduced.

The sudden up-turn in business that Suez brought to the railways came at the most opportune time, because the past eight years had not been good for British Railways and they had experienced a cumulative deficit of £70,000,000 since nationalisation. Furthermore, high levels of investment in rail traffic as opposed to roads had long been questioned in influential quarters, and at Westminster the Conservative-led road-haulage lobby was growing in strength by the mid-1950s.

Above : *Now most people will have seen pictures of strange loads behind a Scammell Scarab at some time, but would this include a caravan.......? In the two pictures seen on this page, we show this type of movement. Firstly with a Western Region 3-ton Scarab in Tyndall Street Goods Yard, Cardiff. It is arriving with a brand-new Fairholme Caravan, whilst another caravan stands on a rail wagon alongside. These locally made holiday-homes were usually forwarded to their destination by rail, and the first part of the journey involved the unusual sight of a Scarab towing the caravan from the works to the rail yard.*

Below: *In the lower view a Shelvoke & Drewry 'Freightlifter' fork-lift truck is shown lifting the load onto a Low-Mac rail wagon. The Freightlifter has a fleet number FT 914D W, and a registered number of LLU 748. Both pictures date from 1956.* both S. Vickery

The strength of the strangle-hold which rail unions could impose on the country also worried the Conservatives and the case for investment in roads had been greatly assisted when the British Transport Commission announced that loans of £256m would need to be made to modernise the railways. They had also announced an annual deficit of £31m for the last financial year! On 4th December 1956 petrol was increased by 1s 5d (7p) per gallon, and it came as a substantial shock to a nation that had previously enjoyed a relatively low cost of motoring. At the same time road haulage costs rose by a further 2.5d (1p) per ton per mile, adding about 1% to the overall price index. On 17th December petrol rationing was introduced, and as might be imagined everyone clamoured for priority - particularly the road hauliers. Within a week the Traders Road Transport Association claimed that many members were having to curtail their businesses or, in many cases, close down completely.

The Minister of Transport, Mr. Watkins, presented BR with a golden opportunity, saying that the 'majority of loads now going by road could easily go by railways, and that if firms would not follow this advice voluntarily he would bring in legislation to enforce it. Two days later a 25% cut in road haulage was ordered affecting just over 17,000 firms operating 100,000 vehicles. The biggest operator, British Road Services, immediately looked at ways to save fuel. Accordingly they announced that as from 3rd January 1957 they had arranged special train services to carry the bulk of their long-distance traffic, and that thereafter their vehicles would be used primarily for local collection and delivery services and for those special journeys that could not be transferred to rail. Pickfords, announced a similar move just two days later.

The railway road vehicle fleet was already in a unique position, and as a result hundreds of new customers went across to their collection and delivery service. A press release was soon issued from Euston, saying 'British Railways wish to point out that they are not fully being used to capacity, and that they would be willing to assist any business experiencing transport difficulties because of the current situation'.

During that first week of 1957 the immediate prospects for the motor and road haulage industries looked very bleak to say the least. The problems of 1956 and the worrying prospect over fuel supplies led to a degree of panic, which was experienced at all levels of the road industry. Immediately after the New Year wide-spread dismissals and short-time notices were announced in the manufacturing sector: Morris laid off 3,000 workers, Rootes Motors went on to a three-day week, whilst at Leyland in Lancashire over 2,000 men were idle, and even Rolls Royce announced cut-backs and a four-day week.

On 8th January *The Times* newspaper championed the cause of the railways with an editorial on page 9, entitled 'Road to Rail' which questioned why greater use was not being made of the spare capacity that British Railways evidently had. In the following days this led to several 'letters to the editor', all of which seemed very eager to quote the inadequacy of rail-freight haulage. Many took great exception to what they thought was a Government transport monopoly, but in reality the Conservatives were far more in favour of private road transport than they were in a nationalised transport industry. However, the national interests submerged political preference at that time.

Critics of the 'Road to Rail' diversion were answered on the 21st January by J.H. Brebner, public relations officer at the BTC who stated 'Individual cases are bound to occur where it is more economical for comparatively small lots of traffic to be carried by road rather than rail. Although conversely there are many instances where railways are cheaper....'. He went on to advise potential users to contact the district commercial officer, or their local goods services manager to outline their requirements. As a special measure facilities would be made for small lots of goods traffic to be conveyed by local and express passenger services; this entailed an urgent memo being circulated for a status return on all available passenger-rated goods stock.

On 22nd January 1957 the BTC decided to try and attract new traffic and duly announced it was to reduce freight charges from 27th January, when there would be cheap rates for users of their railways, road vehicles and canals. The news was welcomed by industry, but still the road lobby claimed that BR were too prone to losing goods in transit. Despite this, questions were now being asked in Parliament as to why the railways and their associated road vehicles could not carry more goods, and for once the road-haulage lobby were silent. The full effect of the diversion of traffic from road to rail began to show in January, which traditionally saw a slight rise in rail traffic as the preference for road transport subsided when the weather was at its worst.

Yet the figures for BR in December had already shown an upward turn in all forms of road delivery traffic. Though we can see this was an immediate advantage to the railways, we must look beyond the short-term benefits and see if their methods of handling this diverted traffic were comparable with the results that would have been achieved by road-haulage. In considering this factor the General Manager of BRS stated, 'The railways did a wonderful job but there was a tendency to overlook the fact that efficiency and cost of movement were not satisfactory by modern standards. For instance in war we can afford a long and heavy pipe-line full of capital goods, but this is out of the question in the modern competitive age.... In this age there is a need to move goods quickly from place to place in order to avoid tying up capital un-necessarily and save handling and packing. It is therefore necessary to have a modern and up-to-date road service, and not only a railway system, which meets some but not all of our requirements.'

In 1948 there were in excess of 1.75 million railway wagons, many of which had been built before the Grouping of 1923. Few were fitted with automatic brakes or screw couplings, so the ability to run fully-fitted express goods trains was woefully inadequate. Along with this fleet BR also acquired some 500,000 private-owner wagons, most of which were fit only for scrap. Despite the proposed modernisation scheme, the introduction of a half-decent rail wagon fleet was still a very long way off. The use of un-fitted freight trains, requiring frequent marshalling, was still widespread in 1957. It was a significant problem which, by its very nature, was central to BR's road delivery service. The problem with the railway's 'bulk-load, slow-progress' policy was, in itself, sufficient reason for the Government to encourage private road-haulage; however, it must be said that this was largely at the urging of industrialists who saw the railways as the *betes noires* of their life.

Above: *The objective of an integrated transport system could be gained by modernisation, but the railways needed to win back customer confidence. Promotional tours were made with specially converted trailers, each of which was lettered with the slogan 'The Complete Transport System'. The display unit body on the Scammell Trailer behind this Austin tractor unit was built by Penman Engineering.* Penman Engineering Ltd.

Below: *Railway delivery vehicles were quite often used for other purposes within BR and, as need dictated, revenue-earning vehicles might be seconded to more urgent non-revenue work. An example of this is seen at Kitchen Hill near Penrith on 8th May 1954, following an accident on the West Coast Main Line. Here we see one of Penrith station's delivery lorries, a Maudslay, arriving at the accident site with packing (old sleepers) from the town's permanent way yard.* The late-Frank Alcock.

The progress towards the introduction of better facilities was there, but it was far slower than both the BTC and BR would have liked. In 1956 the number of freight trains run as fully-fitted had shown a reasonable growth, but during 1957 there was a significant 20% increase, which resulted in marked improvements in reliability and through transit times. Early in the year, when petrol rationing was in full force, the number of fitted goods trains averaged nearly 4,500 a day. This had provided BR with a unique opportunity, as most regions were then able to publish a freight timetable.

The benefits of this were immense, as customers could see at a glance when goods would arrive at a given destination. Indeed as the fuel crisis worsened, many regions were able to offer a service for full-truck loads to be available for delivery at their destination the morning after despatch. In conjunction with a better organised road delivery fleet, an 'Export Express' service was introduced for goods to London Docks in 1956, and later the same service was expanded to ports at Manchester and Liverpool from selected stations in the Midlands. Interestingly, and despite all the adverse complaints about alleged late deliveries, during 1957 not a single load sent by this service missed its ship as a result of a failure on BR's part.

The 'Green Arrow' service which had been re-introduced in 1953 was fully operational by 1957, and for 'full-truck load' customers it offered an almost fool-proof and reliable delivery system. New developments in special rail wagons, such as those built for refractory bricks and bulk powders (like cement), all helped to enhance the railway's reputation as efficient freight carriers.

Even so, the railways could not meet the demand for the small wheeled containers, even though orders for an extra 4,800 were placed. Sadly, inefficiency in fulfiling these orders led to frequent delays in supplying the customer with what he most required. Small wonder that private goods vehicles became increasingly more attractive. Indeed, by the end of 1957 the number of C-licence vehicles had almost caught up with the number of railway wagons.

If only there had been real investment in rail-freight, rather than just a replacement of war-aged stock under the guise of a modernisation programme, the benefits would have been transferred down to the road vehicle services *which had* been substantially developed by this time. In reality, the money they had allowed the railway to spend on its road vehicle fleet was, in so many ways, a complete waste if the rail delivery fleet (on which it depended) was still firmly based on 19th century practice. In reality the railways needed not only to replace exhausted and obsolete stock that had long passed its 'life expectancy', but also substantial development to meet the needs of trade and industry.

Right: *Described as a 'Special Train Crew Bus', this Bedford OLAZ (KXU 332) with an All-Weather body from 1951 appears to have been used in connection with Royal Train duties on the Western Region.* Vauxhall Motors

Below: *Rail wagons in the true sense of the word, with a new 8-ton trailer being transported from the Scammell works. Brian Madeley*

Although passenger traffic was more easily regained, freight needed much more selective attention. In part the answer was to be found in running fully-fitted trains at express speeds, thus eliminating the costly, slow train-miles of conventional rail-freight services; then coupling these to efficient road delivery services. Regretfully the process of building new 'fitted' rail wagons or converting older stock, which was well under way in the early part of 1957 had, by December, been savagely curtailed thanks to the effects of 'capital cuts'. Suez or not, the nationalised railways never stood a chance, they were defeated long before they had begun.

As the *Railway Gazette* wrote at the time, 'Undoubtedly the railways have been, and are, carrying substantial quantities of both freight and passenger traffic which would normally pass by road. There are still some months ahead in which British Railways, by their performance, can show consignors that the enforced switch to rail has been to their lasting benefit.' On 1st May 1957 Parliament approved a lifting of lorry speed restrictions from 20mph to 30 mph.

In connection with this relaxation the Transport Minister, Harold Watkinson, then changed tack by saying 'We have been arguing about it for years and years, and every sort of little pettifogging difficulty has been put into people's way to stop any change being made.' Coupled with this 'official' attitude, we might take the abolition of petrol rationing and the relaxation in commercial vehicle speed limits, at the end of May, as being a Road-hauliers' Charter - railway decline was inevitable.

Yet even in the road transport world, the value of road-rail integration was not being forgotten as Major-General G.N. Russell, the Chairman of BRS pointed out to an audience of transport industry managers in Teesside; 'that the economic advantage had been immense!' When the British Transport Commission published its annual report for 1957, it contained an interesting comment which read: 'The Commission do not wish to see railway traffics protected by bad roads, but they feel it fair to emphasise that railway investment is still only a fifth of the investment in roads.'

The debate of road -v-rail continued down through the latter years of the decade, and eventually a Select Committee of MPs was formed to determine the grounds that the various transport reports, Beeching (railways) and Buchannan (roads), should take. They deliberated for a short while but as far as the railways were concerned these reports eventually brought in two damning conclusions, viz: 'The British Transport Commission has been obsessed with its obligations to the public.' and 'Traffic [specifically that carried by BR road vehicles] should not have been retained at uncommercial rates and fares.'

Sections 217-8 of the BTC report for 1957 further states: 'Nevertheless, and in spite of both sustained and vigorous action by the railway commercial staff, it has not been possible to arrest the gradual diversion of certain traffic formerly carried by rail, to road haulage and particularly to C licensed road vehicles. Some manufacturers and distributors, without perhaps fully weighing up the true economics, withdrew during 1957 traffic which the railways had not failed to handle efficiently during the Suez crisis. Even in coal and minerals the railways have a far from complete monopoly to-day. Some road haulage rates were back to the level of 1948. It only remains to state here that with further advances in the modernisation of railway freight facilities, higher standards of service will enable new freedom in charging to be used more effectively. The experience of 1957 in this respect has at least served to indicate what ground the railways can reasonably expect to recover and consolidate in the future as their equipment is further improved.'

From 1957 to the early 1960s, the decline in freight traffic, which had set in as a trickle in 1948 had turned into a raging torrent by the time Beeching's *Reshaping of British Railways* was published in March 1963. The railway-owned road vehicle fleet, such as the 'Country-Lorry' service was one of the forgotten casualties of his Axe, and it should not be overlooked that for every branch line and station that was closed, dozens of railway freight customers took out their own 'C' licence!

Top Left: *This is a fairly representative picture of the era in question, as a line up of five central London delivery vans are seen one afternoon alongside Marylebone's number 1 platform. The vans in question are Karrier Bantam, Commer, Fordson and BMC.* BR-LMR

Centre Left: *As stated in the text, the small container service operated by BR was found to be exceptionally useful during the Suez crisis, but it is sad to report that BR simply did not have enough to go round. A good example of the small container is seen in this view of two units from the North Eastern Region behind a Bedford OSS used by BR in the Channel Islands.* A. Ingram Collection

Bottom Left: *The larger BD containers will be well known to most readers, and a good example is seen on page 38, whilst the A type container is shown on page 39. Here we see the AFP (A-type Frozen Products) Insulated Container. A large number were used by Birds Eye and Findus frozen foods, and also by ice-cream makers Walls, Lyons Maid, Neilsen and Nestle to achieve national distribution.* Birds Eye-Walls

THE FINAL YEARS
AN ACCOUNT OF OPERATIONS BETWEEN 1957 - 1968

We begin our final section not with the end, but with the beginning of the end as we look at the last 12 years of BR road vehicle operation. In fact we could go back even further than that, as the demise can be traced directly back to 1953, and the Road Haulage Disposal Board's sale of over 46,000 BRS lorries, which took with them the grand dream of an integrated road/rail transport service.

The petrol rationing of the Suez Crisis in 1955-56 created a temporary reprieve for the railways to regain their pre-war dominance of the nation's transport infrastructure, but management of the 1950s were to fail miserably in their attempt to wrestle back this traffic from the roads - if they attempted to wrestle with it at all! By 1956 BRS only retained about 2% of the nation's road haulage vehicles, the railways about 9%, but the initiative given to private enterprise by 1957 was not wasted upon those who would seize the opportunity.

Above: *The final fling of the railway-owned road vehicle delivery fleet will best be remembered for the BMC FG vans, the Commer-Karrier-Dodge walk-thru vans and the Bedford TJ chassis. Here Bedford TJ UAR 687F (fleet no. 2678F) is seen in a yellow livery on its delivery to the Midland Region.* BR-LMR

The industrialists of the 1950s had said they wanted rid of the slow, close-coupled freight trains of the day, and a real social divide emerged as capitalists clamoured for the greater freedom of road haulage. These wishes were ultimately achieved when a new motorway plan was announced to rid Britain of the winding, twisting roads that were legacies of the horse and cart. Yet, next time you travel up the slowly climbing banks of the 2-lane M11, or cross the M62 Trans-Pennine motorway, etc., observe the modern day lorries as they climb laboriously towards the summit; (with barely a couple of feet separating the tail of one truck and the cab of the next) then say that the slow close-coupled freight has vanished for good!

Top Left: *As shown in this picture of a newly delivered lorry at Oldham in April 1965, much of the railway's road motor fleet was delivered from the manufacturers factories to the railway depots direct by rail. These Midland Region Seddon 13:4 tractor units seen here are no exception.* D.Larkin

Centre Left: *During the 1960s there was much more planning in the railway road fleet, but inherent flaws combined to condemn the service to firmly remain a loss-making operation. There were potential bright spots however, and one such example was the integrated transportation services such as cement traffic. This was handled by air-slide rail wagons and dedicated road delivery tankers such as RVY 179, a 1958 BMC FF model. This handled bulk cement transport in the North Eastern region on behalf of Earles Cement.* BR-NER

Bottom Left: *Thank goodness its Guinness! If you are old enough to recall this advert, you may remember when BR used ERF drawbar tankers to pull the famous Irish brew around our streets.* BR

At the end of 1956 the road delivery fleet on BR had increased by 463 units, but these were merely replacements for the 1,265 horse-drawn carts that were sold. Just 206 horses remained, and of these 55 were kept only for shunting purposes. The trend continued in 1957 with only small replacements being made, although as lorries and delivery vans got bigger, they got better; and with diesel engines rapidly coming into fashion the actual capacity of the BR road fleet increased by 7.5% that year. In 1958 significant improvements were made to the rail wagon fleet and, although it had now been reduced to a little over one million vehicles, a total of 215,000 were no more than four years old.

Around 250,000 rail freight vehicles, a quarter of the fleet, now had the continuous brake, many of these also had the benefit of automatic pipe coupling. Nearly 3,000 vans were built or converted for use with pallets and 7,000 'no-door' bulk mineral wagons had been introduced. Yet it was with containerisation that the railways continued to set the lead, and by the end of 1958 47,000 were in service - an increase of 15,000 on the number which came into BR stock on nationalisation a decade earlier. Eighteen different types were in service as BR celebrated its 10th birthday, though the most popular was the 1-ton container, of which no less than 4,000 had been built in just over 2 1/2 years.

Ice-cream and frozen food containers were one new innovation, and as we have mentioned large ice cream companies such as Birds Eye-Walls and Lyons Maid all entered into contracts with BR. To promote container traffic BR held a special exhibition at Battersea Park that autumn, and this was the prelude to the Condor service which would follow in March 1959. There was very little progress in expansion of the road delivery fleet, and although 611 vehicles were purchased, the year ended with the fleet being just one vehicle short of its 1957 total of 15,359. The horse stud had almost come to its useful end, and by 1958 just 75 were left on very selected duties. The story of decline continued in 1959, this time with more marked results as 921 road vehicles were withdrawn, but only 506 new ones were brought in to replace them.

If you look at the declining vehicle figures (which stood at 14,943 vehicles and 34,570 trailers at the end of the 1950s), this decrease now starts to become proportional to the number of station closures that were accelerated in 1959, and then continued apace throughout the 1960s.

Correspondingly, as maintenance of the railways was centralised, more and more 'non-revenue' road vehicles were purchased for this avenue of rail operation. By the end of the decade figures stood at 2,600 stores and materials vehicles, including the ubiquitous permanent way crew bus that started to appear in large numbers. In their own right these vehicles have a fascinating history, and hopefully they will appear as a separate subject study in the future.

The 1960s started the way they were to continue, namely as a period of decline, though at the end of 1960 itself the road fleet had only been reduced by 38 vehicles on the previous year's totals. Carrying capacities were not altering dramatically however, and out of a total of 4,679 rigid motors in the fleet the majority still had less than 2-ton capacity, with a further 1,632 being between 2- and 4-tons. In the larger sizes BR only had 577 vehicles in the 4- to 8-ton range, 11 over 8-tons and eight over 12-tons. In total, the tonnage capacity of the entire fleet was a meagre 78,803 tons. By the end of 1961 this had increased to 80,945 tons, and the fleet numbered 14,817 rigid vehicles and articulated units, 34,726 trailers, 911 cars and 2,257 service vehicles (including an ever increasing number of crew-buses). A year later the vehicle fleet had decreased by 498 lorries or tractor units and 260 trailers - a fact that again directly related to station and branch-line closures.

This trend continued in 1964 with the fleet reducing in a smaller number than 1963, but as the tonnage capacity of the railway wagon fleet dropped by nearly a million tons, there was bound to be a knock-on effect for the road delivery fleet sooner or later. This became apparent in 1965 when 779 rigid vehicles, 1,975 articulated tractors and 1,829 trailers were withdrawn. True some new units were purchased to replace these life-expired members of the fleet, but these amounted to less than half the number of vehicles withdrawn!

Top Right: *On this page we show a series of trailers as used within the railway operation, commencing with this Brockhouse 3-ton van trailer. It is painted in the Carmine & Cream livery, and has a large panel for an advertising poster.* Bill Aldridge collection

Centre Right: *In the brand new bright yellow British Railways livery, we see a well loaded flat-bed trailer at Bradford just after its re-paint. Oddly the picture is dated 9th May 1966, but the paint date on the vehicle declares that it was refurbished on 19th May 1966!!!! The load appears to be boxes of woollen blankets from the Keighley firm of John C. Horsfall & Sons.* BR-LMR

Bottom Right: *In the sand-coloured livery of Rail Freight, complete with its black 'chequer-band marking', this box van was typical of the era. Rear lights had to be transferred from the towing vehicle, and the van had not really moved with the times. It was quite symptomatic of the dated approach taken by the railways.* Brian Madeley.

Containers, meanwhile, continued to increase as the effectiveness of the service was demonstrated and by the end of that year 33,415 were shown in the Capital Stock Account. It is not surprising that the withdrawal figures were so high, especially when we consider that no less than 1,067 railway route miles were closed that year. The next year, 1966, might have been the year when England won the World Cup but on our railways things were far from glamorous as 1,127 route miles and 264 stations closed. As the year ended the road fleet stood at 3,206 rigid vehicles, 7,704 articulated units, and 25,924 trailers - even the container stock had diminished by 1,464 units.

In 1967 the sorry story continued and 305 stations came to their end, 66 marshalling yards closed and 562 route miles were sacrificed as a further part of the Beeching plan. This meant another corresponding reduction in the vehicle fleet and the figures then stood at 2,892 rigid vehicles, 7,253 articulated units and 24,930 trailers.

Unfortunately, unlike most fairy stories, this is not a tale which can be finished with the words ...**and they all lived happily ever after!** In fact it was quite the reverse, as so many of the various parts of the railway freight network closed down for good during the period under review. The first to go was the wagon load traffic, lost to the road haulier partly due to the high cost of transhipping goods between road and rail, but also due to the Government refusing to allow British Railways to compete on fair terms with its competitors.

The Sundries division joined the National Freight Corporation on 1st January 1969, and although it was re-titled National Carriers it retained many of its erstwhile rail trunk links. Along with these links the operation remained committed to the network of new depots set up under the Sundries Plan of 1962, although a number of these depots later changed allegiance and became part of the BRS network. As was noted earlier the Contract Services set up by the railway remained the one saving grace in the whole closure programme, and although the Express Parcels operation lingered on a further 13 years, it too was doomed. The final closure of the express service came in 1981, when the curtain was brought down due to continuing losses and a low level of service offered in comparison to the privately owned carriers; these operators, no longer shackled by the need to obtain A or B licences, competed fiercely with the railways for the parcels traffic and the last nail was finally driven into the coffin of BR's road delivery fleet.

We might ask why this was, especially when the private carriers often charged more per parcel, but the answer is surely found in the fact that these firms were able to offer a much higher level of customer service as regards delivery times and back up services. Perhaps the moral here is that the railway operation had tried to be all things to all men and failed miserably on nearly every count! May it rest in peace!

Top Left: *In the final years the rather attractive Carmine & Cream changed to a sand colour, as shown on this Bedford TK tractor.*

Bottom Left: *This battered Austin tractor is seen at Llantwit Major Station in 1965 with bunker plates for Aberthaw Power Station. S Vickery*

THE ROAD VEHICLE OPERATION - A PERSONAL VIEW

In the first edition of this book, we wrote 'A number of existing 'zonal schemes' were in the process of enlargement to speed the delivery of the sundries/cartage traffic and many more of the cartage agents were in the process of being taken over, giving tighter control over collection and deliveries. There was also the possibility of further road/rail co-ordination between the fledgling British Road Services and the new British Railways, which demonstrated the potential to offer the customer what would now be called "one stop shopping". Many of the successful warehousing and break-bulk schemes originated by the Big Four companies, were extended by BR with railhead distribution services remaining popular.'

On this point John S. Carter felt moved to offer his observations, having worked for both the LNER Road Motor Section and then for BR, from where he retired as a senior manager in 1988, having latterly been involved in the Red Star Parcel operation.

Above: *A York-based Ford Thames Trader 6-cylinder diesel tipper purchased for the Civil Engineers Department, and part of a batch ordered by John S. Carter.* BR NER

'I joined the LNER at York in 1945, as a van boy, and although I did not know it at the time I would soon be working almost exclusively on journey trips to the Terry's chocolate factory. It was quite an honour to get this job, as sweets were still under ration at the time, and the vans were always targets for pilferage. I still have my letter of appointment which gave the job description as 'Van Guard'.

I recall that before joining I had a visit from the LNER's railway police inspector, who went through my school record with a fine-tooth comb, even though he had known me since I was a small boy. He lived at the end of our street, and he often walked to work with my father who was a traffic superintendent. Nothing was taken for granted in those days, and I not only had to prove my own worth, but I also had to live up to my father's good reputation.

It was the start of a very long career, working in an organisation which had a massive potential, but never quite seemed to find its way. I purchased the first edition of this book at an event in the National Railway Museum (NRM) in York, where I got an author-signed copy, and I was impressed with a mass of statistics and facts that the book presented. Having worked in the organisation for over 40 years I was surprised that I was able to learn anything new, but the book just served to show me how vast and widespread it all was, and how great the differences in regional working practices were. I was, however, in total agreement with the statement about zonal schemes, a project with which I was intimately involved between 1956 and 1963.

Having been educated at York Boys Grammar School, it was obvious that I would not stay as a van boy for very long, and at an early stage I was moved into a clerical post in the main goods station, which now incidentally forms part of the NRM. Here I was given the job of handling customer complaints, and one of my first tasks was to investigate a complaint that all the bottles in 14 cases of Dewars Whisky had been carefully opened and their contents replaced with cold tea. The job even involved our chemists at the Doncaster works, who discovered that the tea was of a type supplied by the Scottish Co-operative Wholesale Society. We never caught the culprit, but at least we eliminated the possibility that the theft had taken place in our depot.

In 1956 I had become Zoning Supervisor, and I was working in the Leeds-Bradford area, with the task of re-organising the new distribution arrangements following the formation of the North Eastern Region. As your book pointed out, it was obvious that mass duplication of work was going on, and I found that some ludicrous things were happening. For example, I found that one regular consignment of engineering components were being taken daily by lorry into Hunslet Lane Goods (Leeds) from Beeston Station (ex-GNR), when the regular delivery address was next to Morley Station (LNWR). The distance direct by road was no more than four miles, yet it was taking an average of five days for the consignments to reach their destination by BR.

Another example I could quote was the transport of animal feed stuff between two mills on either side of the Solway Firth, one of these was at Silloth on the old NBR line, the other was near Annan in G&SWR territory. There had once been a bridge across the Solway by which this traffic had originally been sent, but this had long since been demolished, yet we charged the customer a rate based on the fact that we were still shipping traffic across it. The whole position was ludicrous, and we never got to the bottom of it.

Zoning was the answer to a lot of problems, but as soon as we got one scheme going, the rug would be pulled from under our feet, as changes were made again. There was real dedication from managers down to the men on the lorries, but the lack of direction ultimately led to apathy and despair. I hoped that one day we would have the opportunity to get things put on a proper footing but down to the end we were being defeated by both politicians and senior managers; none of whom would ever take any form of initiative because it was more than their job was worth. When you contrast this with the success of private parcels carriers today, it really makes you want to swear!'

Top Left: *An example of how quickly the colour scheme became marked is shown on this 1953 Scammell Scarab in the Rail-Freight livery, which is seen at Leicester on driver training duties.* F. Cassell

Centre Left: *A busy scene at Gateshead sundries receiving shed, with trailers in the centre being loaded from the conveyor. When these were full, they would be placed at the side ready to be removed by the delivery vehicles.* BR NER

Bottom Left: *This Leyland Beaver 12 B/1 model LUW 806, is seen here with a draw-bar trailer, although it was quite a rare beast in the railway fleet.* A. Ingram

Top Right: *Although this Scammell Townsman, EVY 395D, was a recently delivered vehicle, the trailer was from one of the 1949 model Scarabs which the new tractor unit replaced when it entered service on 2nd March 1966.* Huddersfield Examiner

Centre Right: *Still in the North Eastern Region, we see a 1966 British Railways personnel carrier wearing GDN 424D a York registration plate, and a fleet number of EBF 6127N.* BR-NER ·

Bottom Right: *A contract hire vehicle, WBY 119G, fleet no. 6119G W, which was allocated to Exeter. This 1968 BMC model FG van, in its Cadbury livery, is carrying on the tradition of contract hiring to some of the major manufacturers of retail goods.* BR -WR

SAD FACTS

By the end of the second decade of BR's existence, the railways had lost their grand dream of being part of a nationalised integrated transport system. Another 263 stations had gone, leaving a total of just 3,235 stations of which just 2,616 were handling passenger traffic. The network was still a staggering 36,498 route miles; but 748 miles had been closed in 1968 alone, and it is a sad reflection on successive Governments who consistently mismanaged our once great rail transport system. So, at the end of our period under discussion, the rigid motor fleet had shrunk from 5,873 in 1948 to 2,646. It might seem that the number of articulated tractors had gone up from 6,456 to 6,965, and trailers had apparently risen to 24,821 from 23,136 but this superficial glance at the figures takes no account of the fact that these statistics take in all the vehicles that had been purchased to replace horse-cartage. Of the horse stud of 8,231 beasts and its fleet of 24,321 trailers at the end of 1948, the official records show not a single item remaining in 1968. In just five years the tonnage capacity of the rail wagon fleet had gone from 11,348,126 to 7,356,186 - a massive drop of nearly 4 million tons. It was the same story with the passenger seating capacity which stood at 1,809,143 in 1963 but dropped to 1,322,642. It all impacted on the road haulage fleet, and whatever the answer was to the age old question of what to do with the railways, it was not the wholesale closures of the Beeching era. **It was not an asset lost, it was an asset squandered!**

ACKNOWLEDGMENTS

Phil Atkins
Robert Berry
Mike Berry
British Insulated Callendar Co.
British Leyland
British Railways Board
Cadbury-Schweppes Ltd
F Cassell
Colin Green
P G Gomm

Bob Gwynne
H&S Transport Collection
HUB Publishing
Huddersfield Daily Examiner
Arthur Ingram
D Larkin
Peter Love
Brian & Sean Madeley
The Mechanical Horse Club
National Railway Museum

Penman Engineering Ltd.
Phil Roberts
Charles H Roe
Dennis Sherer
Tim Shuttleworth
David Thompson
David Townend
Vauxhall Motors
Barrie C Woods
S Vickery